I See You, Sis

Inspirations from Women of the Bible
Hidden in Plain Sight

Reverend Tisha Williams

Copyright © 2020 by **Tisha Williams**

All rights reserved. No part of this publication may be reproduced, distributed, or transmitted in any form or by any means, without prior written permission.

Scripture quotations marked (CEV) are taken from Contemporary English Version® Copyright © 1995 American Bible Society. All rights reserved.

Scripture quotations marked (CSB) ® are taken from the Christian Standard Bible ®. Copyright © 2017 by Holman Bible Publishers. Used by permission.

Scripture quotations marked (ESV) are taken from The ESV® Bible (The Holy Bible, English Standard Version®) copyright © 2001 by Crossway, a publishing ministry of Good News Publishers. ESV® Text Edition: 2011. The ESV® text has been reproduced in cooperation with and by permission of Good News Publishers. Unauthorized reproduction of this publication is prohibited. Used by permission. All rights reserved.

Scripture quotations marked (KJV) are taken from the King James Bible. Accessed on Bible Gateway. www.BibleGateway.com.

Scripture marked (MSG) taken from *The Message*. Copyright © 1993, 1994, 1995, 1996, 2000, 2001, 2002. Used by permission of NavPress Publishing Group.

Scripture quotations marked (NASB) are taken from the New American Standard Bible ® (NASB), copyright © 1960, 1962, 1963, 1968, 1971, 1972, 1973, 1975, 1977, 1995 by The Lockman Foundation. Used by permission. www.Lockman.org.

Scripture quotations marked (NIV) are taken from the Holy Bible, New International Version. Copyright © 1973, 1978, 1984, 2011 by Biblica, Inc.® Used by permission. All rights reserved worldwide.

Scripture quotations marked (NKJV) are taken from the New King James Version®. Copyright © 1982 by Thomas Nelson, Inc. Used by permission. All rights reserved.

Scripture quotations marked (NLT) are taken from the Holy Bible, New Living Translation, copyright © 1996, 2004, 2015 by Tyndale House Foundation. Used by permission of Tyndale House Publishers, Inc., Carol Stream, Illinois 60188. All rights reserved.

Scripture quotations marked (NRSV) are taken from the New Revised Standard Version Bible, copyright © 1989 the Division of Christian Education of the National Council of the Churches of Christ in the United States of America. Used by permission. All rights reserved.

Renown Publishing
www.renownpublishing.com

I See You, Sis / Tisha Williams
ISBN-13: 978-1-952602-16-0

This book is dedicated to God. Thank You for opening doors and giving me the courage to walk through them.

I also could not have done this without the support of my husband, "The Larry Behind the Lady," and the lessons learned from my parents and the strong women who raised me and stood beside me—my mother, my aunts, and grandmothers Alma and Florence.

This book is also dedicated to my support system, which includes my pastor—Rev. Earl Jones, Sr., who always pushes my train; my First Baptist Church of Bridgehampton family; and the incomparable, amazing women of Lady Nation, who serve as the inspiration for everything that I do.

Lastly, this book is dedicated to the lives of countless women who suffer violence, especially Breonna Taylor, whose murderers at the time of this publishing have yet to be brought to justice. We see you, Sis, and we say your name.

CONTENTS

Foreword	3
Some Women	5
The Hidden Gems	9
God Remembers You	25
God's Woman	43
Who Is She?	63
The Rahab Rehab	87
Go For Yours	107
What's in Your Closet?	123
A Prayer for My Sister	137
About the Author	139
Notes	140

Foreword

Rock star is not a term usually associated with ministers, but when you enter the sanctuary where Rev. Tisha Williams is preaching, you are mesmerized and brought into a reality of the "word became flesh." She is not only a rock star, but also a star for the Rock, Christ Jesus. Her sermons and her teachings have life, and they remind us to have life—and have it more abundantly.

Rev. Tisha is gifted, anointed, assigned, and appointed for this time, so I could not wait for this book, the compilation of her sermons, research, teachings, and insight into the stories of women in the Bible. And now, it's here!

I See You, Sis: Inspirations from Heroic Women of the Bible Hidden in Plain Sight draws us in and leaves us wanting more—wanting to know more, to read more about the biblical heroines and she-roes whom God has used to transform, reform, inform, deliver, rescue, and embrace, throughout God's Word. No longer hidden, these women are brought into full view, and it's great to see. Not only do I see my sister in these pages, but I also see myself: my joys, my struggles, my trials, and my triumphs. From the early leadership of Deborah to the women who carried their "spices" to anoint the body of Jesus, we are with them: at their tables, in their homes, but most of all, in their hearts.

I love the preaching of Rev. Tisha. I love the teaching of Rev Tisha. I love the sermons, so masterfully created and crafted, through which she gives homage to the Creator and makes God's Word *real* for His people. *I love* being in worship with her at First Baptist Church of Bridgehampton, where she is the first woman pastor in its ninety-six-year history. Also, I *love* the response to her authenticity, her warmth, her courage, and her exegesis of reality in God's Word.

And I *love* this book, as I know you will. It will give you a taste of what so many experience every Sunday morning and beyond. If you're like me, you'll find that it's hard to put this book down. You'll want to shout and cry out, "Thank you, Lord, for letting me see myself and my sisters!" *I See You, Sis* is what we've all been waiting for. It's the missing link—the inspiration—needed for transformation.

May you be blessed while reading this book, and transformed as a result of reading it and participating in the workbook that just *keeps it real*. I know I've been transformed, and we're just getting started. May you enjoy these pages, a dynamic undertaking of a dedicated servant of God.

Rev. Dr. Ambassador Suzan Johnson Cook, the third U.S. Ambassador at Large for International Religious Freedom during the Obama administration, is an author, orator, and great admirer of Rev Tisha Williams.

INTRODUCTION

Some Women

In the book of Luke, we read an overview of Jesus' ministry, and it always makes me think of Him going on tour as a rock star would. He was traveling through cities and villages, proclaiming and bringing the good news of the kingdom of God.

I would imagine it was a greatest hits tour. He told the seventy-two disciples to go out ahead of him to the places he was about to appear and promote the tour. He performed such hits as "The Beatitudes," "The Lord's Prayer," and "The Parables."

When the concessions ran out, He multiplied fish and bread and turned water into wine. He gave out VIP—Very Insignificant People—passes to those who desperately wanted to meet Him, like the lame, deaf, blind, and sinners.

With Him on tour was this great group, "The Apostles." We know the apostles—they are almost as famous as Jesus Himself. They need no introduction.

But this is what I find odd and, quite frankly, confusing. Jesus is also accompanied on tour by who Luke describes as "some women" (Luke 8:2). *Some* women? Really? We know the apostles, but what about these women?

It's almost insulting; *some* is so vague. Who were they exactly? The apostles are presented as the premiere Band of Brothers, while "some women" sounds like the random groupies on the tour who followed them from the after-party to the hotel lobby.

And perhaps I see these women as more than just "some women," because I understand the power of women. Think about what just one woman can do. If you ask Michelle Obama, she'll tell you one woman can change the face and ideology of the White House. Elizabeth Warren can shut down a senate floor. It was said that Helen of Troy's beauty could launch a thousand ships.[1] Bathsheba influenced a king to ensure that her son would rule in his place (1 Kings 1:11–31). All these examples prove there is power in *one* woman's decision and action.

If one woman can shape or influence history, what can *some* women do? Imagine the power of *some* women. How can *some* women influence others? How can *some* women change the course of the history they are living in? Whereas one woman can be overlooked, several women cannot be ignored. I wonder, though, how *some* women are viewed by God. Does God see us, and the women mentioned in the Bible, as *some* women—as something less powerful than the key women who changed the course of history?

I'm here to tell you, absolutely, unconditionally, *no*! Though Luke groups them together as *some* women, Jesus doesn't see them as a faceless part of the crowd. How do we know this? Because God takes the time throughout the Bible to give women names and tell their stories. We see women ruling nations, influencing kings, and being an integral part of the Bible from the very beginning.

Women are made in God's image. Genesis 1:27 says,

"So God created mankind in his own image, in the image of God he created them; male and female he created them" (NIV). God made women to represent Himself.

The more time we spend studying the women of the Bible, the more we see we have a lot in common with these sisters from thousands of years ago. This book will take you through the stories of *some* women in the Bible—some well-known, and others easily glossed over—and will explore the powerful ways they were used to change the course of history. At the end of each chapter, workbook sections will help you apply the lessons from these significant women to your life.

Let's dive into the lessons these women learned, for they are just as important today! And who knows, you might just find that all things are possible when *some* women rise up to follow God's great calling—when *you* rise up to be the woman God created you to be!

CHAPTER ONE

The Hidden Gems

> *Soon afterwards he went on through cities and villages, proclaiming and bringing the good news of the kingdom of God. The twelve were with him, as well as **some women** who had been cured of evil spirits and infirmities: Mary, called Magdalene, from whom seven demons had gone out, and Joanna, the wife of Herod's steward Chuza, and Susanna, and many others, who provided for them out of their resources.*
> —**Luke 8:1–3** *(NRSV, emphasis added)*

I love art, especially Italian Renaissance art. Among the famous artists of this era were Michelangelo, Raphael, and, of course, Leonardo da Vinci. An artist, mathematician, inventor, and writer, da Vinci was considered by many to be ahead of his time and is known as the original Renaissance man.

Da Vinci is the artist behind iconic works such as the *Mona Lisa*, the *Vitruvian Man*, and his depiction of *The Last Supper*. As much as I enjoy his work, upon reconsidering the iconic fifteenth-century mural of *The Last Supper*, I immediately thought to myself, *"Something is wrong with this picture."*

Da Vinci didn't miss the details of creating depth by painting a landscape. He was accurate when he placed Jesus in the center of the table because, well, Jesus is the center of everything. Da Vinci accurately captured the chaotic mood of the moment as Jesus had just announced one of the disciples would betray Him. I noticed the detail of a shadowed Judas clenching a bag of money.

And while I enjoyed the features and characterization of each figure in this great work, I still said, "There's something wrong with this picture! Someone is missing."

Maybe it's one of those pictures that requires you to squint and lean forward and pull back to reveal a hidden image. Or perhaps it is more of a Where's Waldo? concept where the main images abound and the one image you're looking for is so embedded in the portrait that it takes severe concentration and a keen eye to find it.

Yes, something was terribly wrong with this painting because someone was definitely missing. As I continued to stare, it became clear this portrait was full of men. Where were the women? Where were the women who had followed Jesus?

The absence of a female presence in this iconic portrait confirmed to me that, in many ways, women have been left out of the picture. Women have been *Hidden Figures* in history long before the 2016 film depicted it.[2]

Where Are the Missing Women?

In my search for why women have been often left out of history, I consulted the Word of God, and I discovered that although women are often left out of history, they are not left out of the Bible. Women, in fact, are named and mentioned in the Gospels. Luke, in particular, highlights Jesus' relationship with women. These women, though present in significant ways, have been relegated to hidden in plain sight status in our study.

Luke, however, shows the significant, poignant, and vital role women played in the ministry of Jesus Christ. Luke tells us of their faith, healing, and discipleship, as well as their part in the birth, death, and resurrection of Jesus Christ. Jesus doesn't see them as specifically "women," rather, He saw them as valuable human beings. If we take into consideration the lesser-known women of the Bible, we see Jesus values all women, just as He values us today. We need to remember all women are welcomed and valued, just as the women in the lineage and ministry of Christ are welcomed and valued.

The Gospel of Luke captures what da Vinci neglected in his painting—women were an integral part of Jesus' ministry. Luke realizes these hidden figures are actually hidden heroes and deserved to be mentioned by name. In Luke's gospel, we see Mary Magdalene, Joanna, and Susanna very much hidden in some aspects of their lives.

Do you ever feel hidden, left out, or inconspicuous? You can be in a room full of people and still feel hidden. You can be the only person in the room and still feel hidden. You can be the only person of color in the room and still feel hidden. You can be the only person at the meeting who actually knows what they're doing and still feel hidden. You can be one of several siblings and feel hidden. You can be the brightest student in the classroom, the greatest singer in the choir, or married for years, and still feel hidden. The reality is that we've all felt hidden.

In a world where perhaps the best of the best often feel like they have to diminish their strengths to fit in with others—for fear someone might be offended or intimidated by their brilliance, beauty, power, courage, skin color, athletic prowess, or our flat-out dopeness—we must remember we are special to Jesus, and His opinion is the only one that matters. We are beautiful roses and should not be forced to be shrinking violets.

Perhaps you feel like the only part of you that people

see is your past, but take heart, though that may be true, Jesus sees every good part of you and sees you wherever you are. God created you uniquely and is not offended by you embracing who you are. You certainly aren't hidden to Him, just like these women mentioned in Luke 8 weren't hidden to Him.

While these women were not necessarily hiding, they were hidden, and as women during that time, they had no choice. Women were expected to put much effort into caring for their homes and families, and it was expected they made few public appearances.[3] Women were under the authority of their husbands and often treated as second-class citizens with few rights.[4] If that wasn't bad enough, women were discouraged from approaching men, and likewise, men generally did not approach women. It is easy to understand how it would seem women were in hiding.

Considering the culture, we can only imagine how many times the disciples and others tried to discourage Jesus from talking to women. Women would have known the cultural rules and expectations and must have felt hesitant to come into His space to learn from Him.

Maybe that's you today. You're not exactly hiding, yet your environment has forced you to remain hidden. You've been discouraged from pursuing your dreams, denied access, and perhaps, talked about negatively by others. You might even feel your mistakes prevent you from coming to Jesus. But all this is no surprise to Jesus.

You may feel worthless, but Jesus sees your beauty hiding in the shadows. Hidden figures are often hidden gems. They are hidden heroes working in hidden spaces while using their hidden talents. You, too, are a hidden gem.

Jesus Found the Hidden Gems

And here in Luke 8, these hidden figures become hidden gems because Luke embedded them in the eighth chapter of his gospel like diamonds in the rough. I use the word *embedded* because if you read through this chapter too quickly, you'll miss them.

The first thing we learn about these women is they were cured of evil spirits and infirmities. Before we learn their names, we learn there had been something wrong with them. And while the Bible specifically states they were *cured* (past tense), they are still identified by what they used to be. The world seeks to define people by what they were and mock what they are trying to become.

Don't you hate when people can only see what you used to be—a drug addict, angry all the time, or drunk? But if we have been discovered by Jesus, He heals us from those things we used to be. Worry less about what you used to be and consider how far God has brought you.

To quote gospel artist Donald Lawrence, "[I] may have some scars, [but] I am healed."[5] The Bible says that "if any man be in Christ, he is a new creature" (2 Corinthians 5:17 KJV). As a new person in Christ, we have walked away from those shameful things we have done in the past. This truth applies to every person, not just women. Jesus healed many, including a blind man, ten lepers, and a lame man.

But for the three women in Luke 8, they used to have infirmities, and now they're following Jesus! Like them, we can now say, "I'm not a hidden figure; I'm a healed figure!"

Though the author forces us to consider these women based on what we think we know about them, we're not told what kind of spirit or which infirmity afflicted them. And yet it's easy to form an opinion and not want to explore their stories any further.

It is dangerous to judge others based only on what they used to be or what we think we know about them. This is true for every person; however, it is often women whose true identity remains hidden. When we do this, we miss out on the blessing of knowing who they really are. These women, the hidden gems among us, such as those in our community, churches, board rooms, and those Luke mentions, make the greatest impact on us. These women are heroic figures!

An Overcomer

Let's look at Mary Magdalene, mentioned in Luke. If the disciples were the Justice League, then Mary Magdalene was Wonder Woman. She is mentioned fourteen times in the Gospels.[6] She was hidden in plain sight. Although she was not talked about in heroic terms, she was indeed a hero; she did what most people, male or female, don't have the courage to do so: she followed Jesus. She moved forward, in spite of the seven demons that once possessed her. She refused to be hidden and instead became heroic.

Mary Magdalene walked with Jesus and the other men through Galilee, and she functioned in circles that were not comfortable for or inviting to a woman like her. She was not only a disciple; she was *the* disciple of all disciples. It was Mary Magdalene who followed Jesus on His last journey from Galilee to Jerusalem (Matthew 27:55), was present at Jesus' trial (Mark 15:40), and saw Him led out to Calvary's fatal mount to be nailed to a tree (John 19:25). It was Mary Magdalene who stood as near the cross as she could to offer comfort, staying loyal to Jesus while He was on the cross while the men fled. Mary Magdalene lingered until the bitter end, prepared the spices for a proper burial of the body, and reached His tomb first at daybreak on the first day of the week (Luke 24:1).

Jesus revealed Himself after the resurrection first to Mary and a group of women, making them the first to carry the good news that Jesus was alive (John 20:14–18).

Mary Magdalene may have had an ugly past filled with demons, but following Jesus transformed her life. An ugly past isn't a reason not to follow Jesus. In Him, you can be a heroic figure like Mary Magdalene.

It doesn't matter what society has labeled you, or what demons you've fought. Keep following Jesus. You're not a hidden figure; you're a heroic figure. Every day you wake up and choose life in the face of death, you're a hero. Every time you declare the victory over your circumstances, you're a hero. Anytime you can look the enemy in the eye and say, "Not today! Get thee behind me" (Matthew 16:23 KJV), you're a hero. When you can wrestle with your demons and still come out victorious, you're a real heroic figure.

A "Secret" Servant

Mary wasn't the only heroic figure in the Gospel of Luke. Joanna was also a hero, even though she was working in a more hidden space. The wife of Herod's steward, Chuza, Joanna was well-known among Herod's servants as one of Jesus's disciples. Naturally, she would talk about Jesus.[7]

But this act of supporting Jesus was dangerous because Herod Antipas was responsible for beheading John the Baptist (Matthew 14:1–12 NLT). When Herod heard about Jesus after beheading John, he said, "John, whom I beheaded, has been raised from the dead!" (Mark 6:16 NIV). Herod wasn't too happy with Jesus.

In short, Herod didn't believe Jesus as Messiah but believed Jesus could work miracles. The Bible says that even the devils believe and tremble (James 2:19 KJV). Likewise, Herod was on the fence in terms of what he really thought about Jesus.

Yet, Joanna lived and worked with the people of Herod's household, and she may have likely talked about Jesus with those who didn't know what to believe about Jesus.

Perhaps someone in your sphere of influence is on the fence where Jesus is concerned. Perhaps a co-worker is wrestling with how they feel about Jesus. Maybe a family member is struggling with whether or not they join you for church as they watch you leave them every Sunday. No matter where you are, someone you know has heard about Jesus and believes in what you say but is wondering about His resurrection power. So it is your job to be a Joanna and live your life to influence their thinking or actions as they come to a decision.

God is looking for some Joannas who will share the gospel no matter where they are or whatever the cost. No matter the hidden space you find yourself in, God is looking for you to serve Him no matter what.

Like Joanna, other Bible characters also served in hidden places. David served God in the cave (1 Samuel 22:1). Daniel served God in the lion's den (Daniel 6). Shadrach, Meshach, and Abednego trusted God in a fiery furnace (Daniel 3). Paul and Silas shared Christ from their dark prison (Acts 26:16–40). In the places they served, they were able to influence the people around them. How much more can you serve in your position today? How does your area of influence change you and others? Even when it is not popular, you can still serve the Lord with joy and show His love. You can have satisfaction just by knowing God sees what you do for Him.

Every day you have the opportunity to share Christ with someone. But will you choose to do so? Will you serve Him no matter what—when it's unpopular, when it's risky, and when it's challenging?

Will you choose to "go and make disciples of all nations, baptizing them in the name of the Father and of the

Son and of the Holy Spirit, and teaching them to obey everything [Christ has] commanded you" (Matthew 28:19–20 NIV)? You do not need to be afraid of what will come when you live out Christ's commission—God is *for* you (Romans 8:31).

The Silent Hero

Not all heroes are outgoing and vocal. Some are silent heroes. The Bible only gives us the name Susanna. The name Susanna is from the root shush, which denotes quiet.[8] The Bible is silent about who she is, and we don't know what she did, we don't know her story, but we do know she had a part in Luke's biblical account. Sometimes the greatest heroes in God's kingdom are the unsung heroes—the people you never really see, but you know are there.

Maybe Susanna was the one who had picked up Peter's fishing pole when he left it in the middle of the floor. Maybe she left a plate of supper for Judas because he was always sneaking off somewhere. Perhaps Susanna sat across the table from Matthew as he counted and accounted for every coin tithed into the ministry. Who washed the dishes after The Last Supper? Perhaps Susanna.

You see, I may not know your name, but God knows your name. He not only knows your name, He also sees everyone silently working behind the scenes taking care of small details—whether for a great moment like the Civil Rights Movement or a huge revival, or for something unnoticed like smiling at an overworked cashier, bringing a meal to a lonely person, or praying for your pastor.

Susanna was there for Jesus taking care of details. Are you there? Are you there when Jesus needs you? Are you there when He requires your service?

Not only did these women—Mary Magdalene, Joanna, and Susanna—use their God-given talents, but also they, along with others, used their financial gifts, as the Bible says: "...and many others, who provided for them out of their resources" (Luke 8:3 NRSV). Jesus paid attention and He recognized their contributions, even if no one else did.

To illustrate, the account of the widow and her two mites showcases how much Jesus cared about the women's contributions.

> *Just then he looked up and saw the rich people dropping offerings in the collection plate. Then he saw a poor widow put in two pennies. He said, "The plain truth is that this widow has given by far the largest offering today. All these others made offerings that they'll never miss; she gave extravagantly what she couldn't afford—she gave her all!"*
> **—Luke 21:1-4**(MSG)

In another account, Jesus was eating at Simon's house when a woman came in with her hair, her tears, and a bottle of oil (Mark 14:1–9). It wasn't much, but what she had she used on Jesus—He said, "Truly I tell you, wherever the gospel is preached throughout the world, what she has done will also be told, in memory of her" (Mark 14:9 NIV).

Women have always been great financial supporters of the church. Why, if it weren't for the dinner sales—women frying chicken, baking macaroni, stewing beef, smothering pork chops, boiling rice, stirring gravy, and candying sweet potatoes—our churches couldn't stand! Jesus multiplied the little boy's lunch of two fish and five loaves, and perhaps his mother was the one who cooked it!

God is using you in ways you and others don't always

see. Continue to give out of your talents and your heart, and watch God bless you. God wants to use your talents, even if you feel hidden.

Jesus saw these hidden women, and He valued them. So, be encouraged; if you are lingering in the shadows, it's time to come out of hiding!

Come Out, Come Out, Wherever You Are!

Although it may be more comfortable to stand on the sidelines or lurk in the shadows, Jesus wants you to venture out into the open spaces so He can use you even more. But if you must hide, hide in the shadow of His wings, hide in the shelter of the Most High, and rest in the shadow of the Almighty (Psalm 91:1 NIV). For it is there that you learn and grow and seek solace. It is there that you are able to release your demons and follow Christ.

Jesus is calling you to release to Him the things holding you back, and He is inviting you to take an active part in loving and serving Him. Jesus will give you the confidence to work where you are best used. If you lean into Him, then you can rest on what He gives you.

If you must hide, play hide and go seek. Matthew 6:33 tells us to "seek ye first the kingdom of God, and his righteousness" (KJV). Seek the kingdom of God first in all you do, and keep God at the forefront as you serve those around you. You may get busy serving in one area, and then get called to another. In this game of hide and seek, you are putting Christ first in your life, seeking His righteousness, and trusting Him to help you live as unto Him in all that you do.

And though you may enjoy living in the shadows, remember you can run, but you can't hide. While you are hiding, know God is an ever-present help in a time of trouble (Psalm 46:1 NIV). He sees your pain, your demons, your fears, and your challenges. Jesus has the power to save you, heal you, and make you like new. When you come into contact with Him, your only response is to worship and serve Him.

It's time to step out of the shadows, lose those demons, and follow Christ. Jesus is saying, "Come out; come out wherever you are!" If these women of the Bible—*some* women—are an example that no one is too broken or too rejected to be used in God's kingdom, then you can boldly come out of wherever you are because God is right there, ready to take your hand. You can come out of poverty, out of sin, out of shame, out of addiction, out of abuse, out of fear, out of bondage, out of confusion, or out of that toxic relationship. Come out, come out wherever you are!

If you can't come out, don't fear, Jesus will bring you out. As the Davidic psalm says, "He brought me up and also out of a horrible pit, out of the miry clay, and set my feet upon a rock, and established my goings" (Psalm 40:2 KJV).

We serve a God who cannot and will not fail. All you have to do is step out with Him and trust Him by faith. You don't have to hide. God has given you everything you need to succeed and to shine for Him (Matthew 5:16).

He brought you out of darkness and into His marvelous light (1 Peter 2:9 ESV). Jesus is that light, the light of the world that was dimmed by death and hidden behind a stone. But on that third day, the Resurrection, I believe God told Jesus, "Come out, come out wherever you are." God saw the hidden then, and He sees them now.

Wherever you are mentally, physically, and spiritually, come out. Jesus has the power to heal and save you and to make you new. Jesus healed Mary Magdalene, Joanna, and Susanna. And because Jesus healed them, they felt compelled to honor and serve Him.

It is the love of Jesus that woos us through the Holy Spirit, and even if we are hidden in plain sight, we can indeed break through the shadows and into His glorious and marvelous light.

WORKBOOK

Chapter One Questions

Question: Describe a time (past or present) when you felt hidden. Did others' actions cause you to feel that way, or were you the one trying to hide? How have you experienced God seeking you out in a time when you were hidden from others? What did that experience communicate to you about God: His heart and nature?

_____
_____
_____
_____
_____
_____
_____
_____
_____

Question: What are some things about your past that you feel have defined you? What should a believer's view of their own (or others') broken past be (1 Corinthians 6:11, 2 Corinthians 5:17)?

_____
_____
_____
_____
_____
_____
_____
_____
_____
_____

Question: Is there a hidden place in your life where you are able to be a witness for Jesus? In what ways are you serving or using your talents and resources to further His kingdom?

_____
_____
_____
_____

_____

_____

_____

_____

_____

_____

_____

Journal: There are times when you need to hide in the shadow of His wings and seek His face, and other times when you should come out of the shadows with boldness and faith. Right now, are you in a season when you need to hide, or when you need to, in faith, step out into the open?

Action: Consider a woman in your church or ministry who has seemed somewhat *hidden* but is actually *heroic*. Spend some time getting to know this lady and encouraging one another. Let her know that God and others see her and value her for her service and devotion.

Chapter One Notes

CHAPTER TWO

God Remembers You

Now there was a certain man of Ramathaimzophim, of Mount Ephraim, and his name was Elkanah, the son of Jeroham, the son of Elihu, the son of Tohu, the son of Zuph, an Ephrathite: And he had two wives; the name of the one was Hannah, and the name of the other Peninnah: and Peninnah had children, but Hannah had no children. And this man went up out of his city yearly to worship and to sacrifice unto the LORD of hosts in Shiloh. And the two sons of Eli, Hophni and Phinehas, the priests of the LORD, were there. And when the time was that Elkanah offered, he gave to Peninnah his wife, and to all her sons and her daughters, portions:

But unto Hannah he gave a worthy portion; for he loved Hannah: but the LORD had shut up her womb. And her adversary also provoked her sore, for to make her fret, because the LORD had shut up her womb. And as he did so year by year, when she went up to the house of the LORD, so she provoked her; therefore she wept, and did not eat. Then said Elkanah her husband to her, Hannah, why weepest thou? and why eatest thou not? and why is thy heart grieved? am not I better to thee than ten sons? So Hannah rose up after they had eaten in Shiloh, and after they had drunk. Now Eli the priest sat upon a seat by a post of the temple of the LORD. And she was in bitterness of soul, and prayed unto the LORD, and wept sore. And she vowed a vow,

> and said, O LORD of hosts, if thou wilt indeed look on the affliction of thine handmaid, and remember me, and not forget thine handmaid, but wilt give unto thine handmaid a man child, then I will give him unto the LORD all the days of his life, and there shall no razor come upon his head...
>
> And they rose up in the morning early, and worshipped before the LORD, and returned, and came to their house to Ramah: and Elkanah knew Hannah his wife; and the LORD remembered her.
> —*1 Samuel 1:1-11, 19*(KJV)

If the basic purpose of memory is to keep a record of information for a period of time, then one really interesting thing about human memory is how selective it is. We're often extremely good at *forgetting*. We forget to pick up our kids, and we forget where we put our keys. We forget to turn off the stove, or we forget to pay bills. Sometimes, we even forget to eat! And yet, while we can forget to pick up milk on the way home, we never forget the hurtful remark someone made about us two years ago.

While these events sound like major or minor defects, when you consider we can only pay attention to so many things at once, forgetting is a tactic we have developed to help us focus on the things immediately relevant and important. By only focusing on what is immediate or important, we concentrate on what really matters to us among the endless clutter of our everyday lives. Forgetting something is like throwing out old junk from your closet to make room for new stuff.

Total Recall

I am so grateful that God's memory is not like ours. God is not in the habit of forgetting, but rather, Psalm 115:12 tells us, "The LORD remembers us and will bless us" (NIV). God remembers every finite detail about us, and

He cares. If He remembers the sparrow that falls, then He will surely remember us in our situation (Matthew 10:29).

Unlike us, God has never forgotten to pick us up when we feel scattered. God has never forgotten to turn things down when we are being consumed. God has never forgotten to feed us when we are hungry. It is God's nature to remember.

Though our minds are like leaking sieves, God's mind has *total recall*, that is, "the ability to remember with clarity every detail of the events of one's life or of a particular event, object, or experience."[9] Psalm 9:12 tells us that God "remembers ... the afflicted" (NIV). For God even remembers the sparrows so that "not one of them is forgotten by God" (Luke 12:6 NIV).

And throughout the Bible are several examples of people who have been beneficiaries of God's perfect memory. God remembered Abraham (Genesis 19:29) and rescued Lot (Genesis 19:1–29). God remembered Noah in the midst of the flood (Genesis 8:1). God remembered Samson and gave him the strength to defeat his enemies (Judges 16:28–30). God remembered the thief on the cross and gave him a home in paradise (Luke 23:40–43). From these, we really see that God doesn't simply "remember," God has total recall.

First Samuel 1 begins with Elkanah, Hannah's husband, performing his rightful duty at Shiloh as he traveled to the place where the men went up yearly "to worship and to sacrifice unto the LORD of hosts" (1 Samuel 1:3 KJV). More specifically, Elkanah and his wives and family were there to celebrate the Feast of Tabernacles, which was a time of great rejoicing in God's blessings, much feasting, offering to the Lord, and grand festivities.[10]

The Feast of Tabernacles was similar to celebrating Christmas and giving thanks for what they had. However, Hannah was feeling discouraged. Year after year, she was forced to celebrate and be grateful when she was grieving and in pain. She was going through the motions of participating in this feast.

Hannah was grieving because she no children. Her womb was barren, unable to produce fruit. Hannah was broken and felt worthless based on her inability to produce children. Not only that but also she must have felt the emptiness of not cradling her own child.

In contrast, Hannah can be viewed as a mother: the faithful mother, the prayerful mother, the hopeful mother.

But, I don't want you to think of Hannah as a mother or a wife. Think of her simply as a woman.

Hannah, a woman like so many of us today, perhaps, felt barren, empty, and useless. Like Hannah, we want so desperately for God to fulfill our dreams. In our prayers, we cry out to God, "Remember me!" These two simple, yet powerful words were Hannah's plea as well. It is safe to assume Hannah, like us at times, believed somewhere along the way God had forgotten her.

Remember Me

If we are honest, we will admit we sometimes believe God has forgotten about us. We become so desperate and blinded that we think we are alone and worthless. Maybe that's how you're feeling right now. Perhaps, you believe God has forgotten you because you haven't reached those career, financial, relationship, or familial goals yet. Maybe you think God has forgotten you in the midst of trying and difficult circumstances. Maybe you are in deep pain and grieved in your spirit, and the only prayer you can pray is: *"Lord, remember me."*

If that's you today, then be encouraged that you have truly believed an untruth because God remembers you. Allow God to take off the blinders so you won't feel forgotten. But let this be a comfort that while God remembers you, some things you must not forget.

You can't forget how good God is. As 1 Samuel 1:4–5 says, "And when the time was that Elkanah offered, he gave to Peninnah his wife, and to all her sons and her daughters, portions: But unto Hannah he gave a worthy portion; for he loved Hannah: but the LORD had shut up her womb" (KJV). In the midst of barrenness, God always provides in other ways.

An article from the website *Walking in Truth* gives a powerful description of the feast and of the significance of the portions Elkanah offered to the Lord.[11] During this feast, the sacrifices were served in specific ways. Elkanah brought his peace offering to the priest. The article described the sacrifice this way:

> ...the blood was poured out at the foot of the altar ... the fat burned on the fire ... the breast and right shoulder were given as a portion to the priest ... and the rest was shared by the offerer with his family, friends, and guests. Everyone was given a part or portion-the greater part being given to the offerer-and then eaten at a social feast before the Lord.

In verses 4–5, something very interesting happened. Elkanah gave Peninnah and her children "portions," but he gave Hannah a "worthy portion." But what is the difference between a portion and a worthy portion? The Hebrew word for *worthy* in this passage is the word *'aph* which means "a double portion."[12]

What was the significance of giving Hannah a worthy portion and Peninnah only a single portion? The article goes on to explain:

> It is important to understand that there was an Eastern custom whereby the host of the feast would place before his beloved or distinguished guest a "worthy portion" in

order to show him great regard or to signify that he was most valued. In the presence of all his guests, Elkanah wanted to distinguish Hannah above the others. It was his desire to prove his special love for her and to comfort her in her particular affliction of not being able to bear children. Hence, he ordered the choicest piece of the sacrifice for her.

And not only did he give her the choicest piece, but Elkanah also did so in the presence of Peninnah.

In addition, Peninnah's portion was given to her, her sons, and her daughters, but Hannah was offered a portion for just herself. Perhaps it illustrates that what God has for you is only for you, and He responds to us in different ways based on exactly what we need at the time! In this one act, Elkanah compensated Hannah for the lack in her life with a double portion of his offering.

You may be lacking in one area but be encouraged; God sees the deepest part of you, and He desires to fill that void. But when it is impossible at the moment or simply not the right time, He makes up for it in another area of your life. He may give us more mercy when we are broken, or He may send people to us when we need extra help.

Take, for example, the human body. Research done by scientists and specialists discovered that when a person lacks one of the senses, they improve in the other senses as a result of learning new behavior.[13] In the absence of vision, blind people pay attention to auditory cues and learn how to use them more efficiently. There is growing evidence that people who are missing one sense don't just learn to use the others better. The brain adapts to the loss by giving itself a makeover. If one sense is lost, the areas of the brain normally devoted to handling that sensory information do not go unused—it gets rewired and put to work processing other senses. In other words, your body compensates for what is lacking.

God is an expert in compensating for what you lack the most. In the Old Testament, "when the LORD saw that Leah was unloved, he opened her womb" (Genesis 29:31 NRSV). God compensated for Leah's lack of love by giving her someone to love! In the New Testament, when Jesus was preparing the apostles for His departure from the earth, He told them, "Nevertheless I tell you the truth; It is expedient for you that I go away: for if I go not away, the Comforter will not come unto you; but if I depart, I will send him unto you" (John 16:7 KJV). Although the disciples would miss Jesus or Emmanuel—God *with* us, they were compensated with the Holy Ghost—God *in* us!

How did God compensate Hannah? He showed her grace and favor. She was sitting at the feast with the choicest portion—a symbol of honor. But she did not have any children around her, which was her deepest desire. Hannah may not have had what she wanted, but she had grace and favor at that moment.

And that is how it is with us. People may have expectations of what you are meant to accomplish, but God loves you simply because of who you are. And perhaps people only want to be around you for your achievements. But God takes you as you are. Your popularity does not determine how much God loves you. People may not appreciate or even notice your talents, but God does. God may not give you everything you want, but He gives you grace and favor (Psalm 84:11). And, not only does He give us this, but He also remembers us. What more could we want?

In all our grief and pain, we become so focused on what we don't have that we tend to forget how good God is and just how much He gives us each day. We can imagine it must have been hard for Hannah to remember how good God was because her external circumstances seemed against her.

How true is that for us? How often do we forget how God holds us in the palm of His hand and wants only the very best for us (Isaiah 51:16 CEV)? If we want God to remember, we must remember several things.

Ignore the Enemy

First, we must remember to ignore the enemy and focus on God. Scripture tells us in 1 Samuel 1:6–7 that Hannah's "adversary also provoked her sore, for to make her fret, because the LORD had shut up her womb. And as he did so year by year, when she went up to the house of the LORD, so she provoked her; therefore, she wept, and did not eat" (KJV). Peninnah provoked her *as* she went to the house of the Lord.

Peninnah, whose name means "Pearl" or precious stone,[14] was valued but not favored. Value is what man *thinks* you are worth, but favor is what God *knows* you're worth. Peninnah was valued because of what she could do—she could produce children, and in those days, having children was a badge of honor, a symbol of status.

In contrast, Hannah was favored simply because of who she was. Hannah was gentle as she approached the Lord in prayer. She was quietly weeping before the Lord. The Bible does not say Hannah was unkind to Peninnah.

But if I can reflect on Peninnah for a minute, imagine how she must have felt. Though Hannah felt like she was forgotten by God (1 Samuel 1:11), it seems as if Peninnah was forgotten by Elkanah even though she had borne him children. Hannah did not have a child, and Peninnah did not have her husband's attention. Each woman felt broken in their own way. And when we consider Peninnah, we often overlook her pain and how it could have influenced her destructive behavior toward Hannah. We all have our struggles to contend with—it is how we respond to those struggles that define who we are.

Year after year, Hannah was forced to celebrate, and year after year, she was dealing with the torment of Peninnah. The Bible indicates Peninnah tormented and teased Hannah because she was barren until Hannah cried and could no longer eat. Peninnah gloated because she had children, and Hannah had none (1 Samuel 1:6–7).

Hannah must have felt like a failure. Here was another year, watching as Peninnah's children ran around the table instead of her own babies. Another year of watching Elkanah bounce *Peninnah's* children on his knee. Truly, Hannah must have felt forgotten. No wonder she didn't like going to these holiday gatherings.

And truth be told, some of us can relate. Sometimes the circumstances or treatment from other people can make you feel like a failure. Year after year, and you wonder, *"God, You're blessing everyone else. Did You forget about me?"*

But not only that, let's look at *when* Peninnah provoked her: "…when she went to the house of the LORD" (1 Samuel 1:7 KJV). Is it just me, or does the enemy always try his best to mess with us on Sunday morning when we're trying to get to church? The car won't start. The kids are having a tantrum. You can't find your keys. Or you spill something on your shirt. None of us welcome the enemy distracting us from God, but we each must stay focused on God so as not to overlook God's grace and favor on us.

Hannah was allowing Peninnah to distract her from God and His love for her. When Elkanah sees Hannah in her grieved state, he is concerned as a husband should be and says to her, "Hannah, why do you weep? … Why do you not eat? Why is your heart grieved? Am I not better to you than ten sons?" (1 Samuel 1:8 NKJV).

In other words, Elkanah was saying, "Hannah, I see you are grieved because you do not have children but know that you have a man who loves you." We can only imagine how tenderly he spoke this to her. It's as if he were trying to convey that Peninnah may have had children, but Hannah had an equally precious thing—the genuine love of her husband.

And just like Elkanah had said all this to Hannah, I can hear God saying to us today, "Why are you crying, and why is your heart grieved? Am I not better than anything else in the world to you? You have a God who loves you! Am I not better to you than a job or money? Am I not better to you than a man? Am I not better to you than a title or degree? Am I not better than a bank account? Am I not better to you than a mother or father? Am I not better to you than a friend? Am I not better than drugs? Am I not better to you than you have been to yourself?"

Why are you crying? Why are you grieved? You have a God who loves you! You can change the *am I not* to the *I Am*! Because God the *I Am* is everything. And you are the daughter of *I Am*.

Though we may not have money, we have a God who loves us. Though we may not have success, we have a God who loves us. Though we may not have cars and houses, we have a God who loves us. Why are we crying, and why is our heart grieved? We may not have what we want, but we do have everything because we have a God who loves us and who is above everything we could ever ask for or even think about (Ephesians 3:20).

Those words from God are a lot to process, and perhaps Elkanah's words gave Hannah a revelation, too, because the Bible indicates that "Hannah rose up after they had eaten in Shiloh, and after they had drunk" (1 Samuel 1:9 KJV). I picture her standing up, dusting herself off, taking one last sip of wine for courage, wiping her eyes and squaring her shoulders, then giving Elkanah a weary smile and sticking her tongue out at Peninnah (just kidding). I picture her heading toward the temple, saying to herself, *"If I want God to remember me, I must remember God!"*

Hannah was only barren in one area of her life, and she

had determined not to let that one area of barrenness define her as a person or define the rest of her life. The rest of her life was fruitful. She was childless but not loveless. She was childless but not praiseless. She was childless but not prayerless. She was childless, but she wasn't godless. She had a God who loved her.

Even though she couldn't give birth to a new life, she could speak life! She went to the temple, "and she vowed a vow, and said, O LORD of hosts, if thou wilt indeed look on the affliction of thine handmaid, and remember me" (1 Samuel 1:11 KJV). So she said, "Lord, remember me!" As you apply it to your situations, your barrenness does not define you! Whatever you lack in your life does not have to define you!

We Must Do Our Part

Second, we must remember we can't forget to do our part. There are actually two parts to doing our part—a spiritual part and a physical part.

The spiritual part is in this verse: "And they rose up in the morning early, and worshipped before the LORD" (1 Samuel 1:19 KJV). They rose up early in the morning. It was a new day. Hannah was crying yesterday—but today, she was worshiping God. How many people are ready for a new day? Hannah worshiped the Lord. At some point, you have to go from wallowing to worshiping, because let me tell you what worship says to God. It says I trust You when I can't trace You. While You're preparing, I'm going to keep praising. You're working it out, and I'm not worried.

The physical part is also in verse 19: "...and [they] returned, and came to their house to Ramah: and Elkanah knew Hannah his wife" (KJV). Here, faith without works is dead (James 2:26 KJV). We can't expect to accomplish anything if we don't put forth the effort. If you want to be an entrepreneur, you need a business plan. If you want a promotion, start working on your degree. Do you want financial freedom? Then create a budget and stick to it. You have to do your part because when you do your part, God will do His part.

It's About God's Timing, Not Ours

Third, we can't forget God's timing. It also says in 1 Samuel 1:19 that "the LORD remembered her" (KJV).

Sometimes God will put things in your life that make no sense just to get you where He needs you to be. God allows things that don't feel right to cross your path. He allows circumstances, challenges, and obstacles on your path. And you're probably saying to yourself, *"God has forgotten about me."* No. He didn't forget about you. He's just waiting for the right time to show up and show real results in your life.

When we read the book of 1 Samuel, it begins with one key word: *now!*

Perhaps it's God's way of saying, I know what you've been through, but ... *now!* I have heard you crying, but ... *now!* You have been in pain, but ... *now!* You have experienced trials and tribulations, but ... *now!* You have suffered many sleepless nights, but ... *now!*

Now is faith. Now is the same faith as in Hebrews 11:1, where faith is the substance of things hoped for, the evidence of things not seen. *"Now* is the acceptable time; see, *now* is the day of salvation" (2 Corinthians 6:2 NRSV). "Come *now*, and let us reason together" (Isaiah 1:18 ESV). "There is therefore *now* no condemnation to them which are in Christ Jesus" (Romans 8:1 KJV).

The Best Vessel

It was never that Hannah couldn't conceive; it just wasn't time for her to conceive. Remember, just because God shut *up* her womb, doesn't mean He shut *down* her womb. Hannah couldn't see the big picture and didn't know God's plans.

Sometimes when we're praying and waiting for a long-awaited blessing, we feel as though God has shut it down rather than shutting it up. But there's a difference. When God shuts things down, He's saying no; when He shuts things up, He's saying: *not yet; just hold on a little while longer. It's not time yet; I know best.*

And it's also a matter of protection because when God shuts things up, what you are meant to birth can't get out. But that also means nothing is getting in! God is using this shut-up season to *shut out* anything that threatens to destroy His plan for you. No weapon formed against you shall prosper (See Isaiah 54:17). God is covering and protecting whatever He is shutting up. Because, at the appointed time, He will use you for His glory. So, don't worry because while you're shut up, God is fixing up! And God was fixing things up for Hannah.

God wanted a great judge for His people. Samuel was that judge. And for Samuel, this great judge, God wanted the best vessel, Hannah, to birth him. It's not that you won't get your dream job, but God needs the best vessel. It's not that you won't get married; God needs the best vessel. It's not that you won't find the home you've been praying for, but God needs the best vessel.

Many things seem impossible. But God always chooses the best vessels to carry out His will. God sent us a perfect vessel. His name was Jesus. And He *is* the best vessel because Jesus can compensate for anything lacking in your life. If you lack friendship, there's no friend like Jesus, as He sticks closer than any brother (Proverbs

18:24); If you lack peace, Jesus says, "Peace I leave with you; my peace I give to you" (John 14:27 NRSV). Do you lack joy? Oh, but "the joy of the LORD is your strength!" (Nehemiah 8:10 NIV). Do you lack eternal life? The Bible says Jesus is the way, the truth, and the life (John 14:6)!

With Him, there's no lack, no barrenness in your house, your mind, your heart, or your life. If you want it, God's got it!

Often, like Hannah, we tend to fixate on what we don't have or what God didn't do for us, so much so that we forget to consider what God has done for us. It's a miracle each time we wake up in the morning. God keeps us in the right frame of mind as we go about our days. When everyone else forgets about us, God has total recall. God remembers you, He's got you, and you have a direct connection to God anytime you need Him. He promises never to leave you nor forsake you (Hebrews 12:5).

The Bible gives no indication if Hannah ever prayed before that moment in the temple. But at that moment, she chose not to be defined by her circumstance, and instead, chose to trust and to watch God move as soon as she said, "Remember me." Whatever you want or need, just remember: God's got it because He never forgets.

WORKBOOK

Chapter Two Questions

Question: Describe an "I will never forget" moment when someone said or did something (good or bad) that impacted you. What made this moment so unforgettable? Have you ever felt forgotten by God? When and why?

_____
_____
_____
_____
_____
_____
_____
_____
_____
_____

Question: In what ways has God compensated your lack in one area of your life with a worthy or double portion in another area? How has He given you Himself and His love and attention, even as you wait for Him to fulfill your desires?

_____

_____

_____

_____

_____

_____

_____

_____

_____

Question: Do you have someone in your life who provokes and belittles you, disrupting your worship and making you feel like a failure? Do you have an Elkanah—someone who loves and favors you unconditionally? How can you be an Elkanah for someone else in your life? How can you avoid the competitiveness and jealousy that can potentially destroy someone else's faith?

_____

_____

_____

_____

_____

_____

_____

_____

_____

_____

_____

Journal: *We may not have what we want, but we do have everything because we have a God who loves us and who is above everything we could ever ask for or even think about.* How is God more than enough for you, even in your lack? Journal about His all-sufficient presence and provision in your life.

Action: As you face whatever you feel you are lacking, how will you go from wallowing to worshiping? What steps do you need to take in faith to not allow any feelings of being forgotten to hold you back? Write out your worship and action plan and *do it*.

Chapter Two Notes

CHAPTER THREE

God's Woman

The words of King Lemuel, the prophecy that his mother taught him. What, my son? and what, the son of my womb? and what, the son of my vows?

...Who can find a virtuous woman? for her price is far above rubies. The heart of her husband doth safely trust in her, so that he shall have no need of spoil. She will do him good and not evil all the days of her life. She seeketh wool, and flax, and worketh willingly with her hands. She is like the merchants' ships; she bringeth her food from afar. She riseth also while it is yet night, and giveth meat to her household, and a portion to her maidens. She considereth a field, and buyeth it: with the fruit of her hands she planteth a vineyard. She girdeth her loins with strength, and strengtheneth her arms. She perceiveth that her merchandise is good: her candle goeth not out by night. She layeth her hands to the spindle, and her hands hold the distaff. She stretcheth out her hand to the poor; yea, she reacheth forth her hands to the needy. She is not afraid of the snow for her household: for all her household are clothed with scarlet. She maketh herself coverings of tapestry; her clothing is silk and purple. Her husband is known in the gates, when he sitteth among the elders of the land. She maketh fine linen, and selleth it; and delivereth girdles unto the merchant. Strength and honor are her clothing; and she shall rejoice in time to come. She openeth her

> mouth with wisdom; and in her tongue is the law of kindness. She looketh well to the ways of her household, and eateth not the bread of idleness. Her children arise up, and call her blessed; her husband also, and he praiseth her. Many daughters have done virtuously, but thou excellest them all. Favor is deceitful, and beauty is vain: but a woman that feareth the LORD, she shall be praised. Give her of the fruit of her hands; and let her own works praise her in the gates.
> —***Proverbs 31:1-2, 10-31***(KJV)

I am in conflict with the Proverbs 31 woman and the unrealistic ideals that have grown to embody her. Such expectations have challenged women for far too long.

Throughout the country, at almost every women's luncheon, every fashion show, every platform service, every Mother's Day, or any other women's meeting, the Proverbs 31 woman—this virtuous woman, this wife of noble character—is usually at the center (Proverbs 31:10 NIV).

I've been married almost twenty-three years, and, at best, my husband can say I am a character—forget noble character! And while I realize this poem in Proverbs, this ode to the virtuous woman, was meant to inspire women, I must admit she makes me feel a bit *less than* and, quite frankly, she makes me question if I'll ever hit the mark of perfection. Perhaps you feel the same way at times.

Even the author of the text begins the section by asking, "Who can *find* a virtuous woman?" Yeah, who indeed? Does she really exist? This word *find* is the same word used in Genesis when no suitable helper had yet to be *found* for Adam (Genesis 2:20 NIV).[15] And do you know why that helper wasn't found? Because she didn't exist yet. God had yet to create her!

So what about the case with the virtuous woman? She's like a unicorn, Bigfoot, or the loch-ness monster. I'd also argue that you'd have just as hard a time finding her as you would with finding any of them. Perhaps, you too feel a bit of frustration, knowing how hard it is to attain the height and depth of the Proverbs 31 woman. If you're somewhat frustrated with the way the P31 lady has been used in modern Christianity to hold women to an unattainable standard, know that I'm slightly uncomfortable with how the entire book of Proverbs talks about women.

The purpose of Proverbs is to teach people how to live a sensible, disciplined life. In addition, Solomon, who wrote most of the book, provides instruction for several areas, including youth, self-control, honesty, family, money, marriage, and, of course, wisdom—the overarching theme of the entire book.

And as if all these topics aren't enough, Solomon has a great deal to say about women, with one of the most popular verses being Proverbs 18:22: "He who finds a wife finds a good thing and obtains favor from the LORD" (NKJV). Yes, everybody knows that verse. But, except for a few edifying scriptures about women, Solomon is actually quite hard on the female gender.

Solomon advises to stay away from several types of women: the unfaithful, who tries to lead you into adultery by her pleasing words (Proverbs 5); the sinful, who, although beautiful, may cost you your life (Proverbs 5:5); the prostitute, who will treat you like a loaf of bread (Proverbs 6:26); the loud and stubborn woman likened unto foolishness, who never stays at home (Proverbs 9:13–15); and the strange, unsaved woman (Proverbs 2:16–17).

Furthermore, Solomon says a woman without discretion is like a gold ring in a pig's snout (Proverbs 11:22). He warns that a disgraceful wife is like a disease in her husband's bones (Proverbs 12:4). He advises it is better to live on a corner of the roof than in a house with a quarrelsome wife (Proverbs 25:24). Solomon likens a wife's quarreling to a continual dripping of rain (Proverbs 27:15). Yes, sis, women are raked across the coals.

Who Is This Virtuous Superwoman?

To add insult to injury, Proverbs concludes with a glowing poetic description of the perfect woman. Not one-liners like those used to describe the ill-fitting other women, but this perfectly-fitting woman gets twenty-two verses. This woman was perfect in her character and description.

In this poem, the author wrote it as an acrostic, which begins each verse with a successive letter of the Hebrew alphabet. The acrostic is used to help you remember something, which means this woman—with claim to her own designated chapter—is meant to be unforgettable. Next, look where the verses describing her are positioned: Not scattered throughout the book like the other women but prominently featured as the epilogue of Proverbs.

And, as if that's not enough, look at who she is and what she does. She is an outstanding woman of amazing capabilities, an excellent wife and mother, manufacturer, importer, manager, realtor, farmer, seamstress, upholsterer, philanthropist, socialite, entrepreneur, and advisor. That's just who she is.

Now, let's look at what Scripture says this woman does. She seeketh, worketh, bringeth, considereth, girdeth, strengtheneth, perceiveth, layeth, stretcheth, maketh, sitteth, delivereth, openeth, looketh, gets, praiseth, and she excelleth. And to top it all off, she keeps herself and her kids looking good, and she satisfies her husband because with her, "he will not lack anything good" (Proverbs 31:11 CSB). She maketh me sicketh—because if that isn't perfection, I don't know what is.

Let's be real. As women, the best most of us can hope for on any given day is to make sure we are wearing matching shoes or to remember to put on deodorant. The character and ambition litany about this perfect Proverbs 31 woman puts a great deal of pressure on us imperfect women, and particularly for those women in leadership.

Therein lies the conflict. When we consider this virtuous woman and all she does and all she is, we are forced to come to terms with all that we are not. I don't know about you, but I don't feel like a superwoman! And the truth is, we may never be a superwoman—and maybe that's not what God wants from us.

I decided to confront this conflict head-on and deal with this virtuous superwoman. But let me tell you something, she has been dealing with me. What I found is while the Proverbs 31 woman is the epitome of perfection, we're all like her in more ways than we think. She, like us, had her own story, in which she needed support, and when she had a struggle, God gave her strength. The virtuous woman trusted in God to do the work in and through her.

Can a Shameful Woman Become Virtuous?

Now when we think about the virtuous woman and all she represents, we don't often think about who, specifically, she might have been. However, many ancient rabbinical commentators identified Lemuel as being Solomon.[16] And Proverbs 31:1–2 offers insight into this because the chapter opens with this introduction: "The words of King Lemuel, the prophecy that his mother taught him. What, my son? and what, the son of my womb? and what, the son of my vows?"

While we can't know for sure who Lemuel is, let's say the ancient rabbinical commentators were right, and "Lemuel" was just a special name given to Solomon by his mother to remind him and possibly herself that he was "of God."

If, in fact, Solomon was Lemuel, then we must deduce that the mother giving this sage advice to her son about "the perfect woman" was none other than Bathsheba.

And therein lies the pickle—because if that's the case,

I'm sure you're all asking the same question I would: "Who is Bathsheba to be giving such wholesome advice about virtuous women?" She is often thought of as an adulteress, a seductress, whose husband was off fighting a war while she had an affair with King David. Far from virtuous, wouldn't you say?

So, what qualified Bathsheba to give sage advice to her son on how to find a virtuous woman, or to tell other women how to be virtuous? This is where I got schooled!

The biblical story we remember most about Bathsheba is her promiscuous action with King David. Bathsheba was on her rooftop, as was customary for the day, taking a bath required by Levitical law. Scripture recounts "it happened, late one afternoon, when David arose from his couch and was walking on the roof of the king's house, that he saw from the roof a woman bathing; and the woman was very beautiful" (2 Samuel 11:2 ESV).

David saw her from the higher vantage point of his palace, inquired about her, and sent his messengers to get her (2 Samuel 11:2–4). And guess what? Married and all, she went along with it. Why? Because in those days, when the king called, you didn't refuse. Disobeying the king's orders could have meant death. Some could argue that Bathsheba did what she had to do to stay alive. We can only suppose she tried to make the best possible choices in the midst of a less-than-ideal situation.

Bathsheba encouraged her son to find the right woman, a virtuous woman, perhaps in the hope he wouldn't make the same mistakes as his father, David. In any case, this is not advice Solomon (Lemuel) offered from his own wells. Rather, this was advice pressed upon him out of the hard experience of a wise mother.

I imagine this conversation was one of those rare moments a child finds with his or her mother, that is when the house is quiet and there's a chance meeting at the kitchen table. It's not set up or pre-planned; it happens organically.

It's not the premeditated speech for the day, intended to compel her child to behave. And it's not the staccato speech she yells while she's not sparing the rod. No. This conversation is the rare but tender moment that happens unexpectedly when Mama drops her pearls of wisdom, which is the advice you remember for the rest of your life.

And if Bathsheba really is the one offering this advice for the description of the virtuous woman in Proverbs 31, we can find hope in that. Despite the circumstances that led her to become David's wife and Solomon's mom, she didn't let it keep her from stepping up as a virtuous woman.

Your Past Doesn't Define Your Present

We tend to judge people—like, perhaps, the virtuous woman in Proverbs 31—based on what we see now, never considering they have a background story.

Someone who is virtuous now might have started out like Bathsheba, with a past deemed shameful or a less-than-perfect life story. But we must not let our past define our present, and we must not judge someone else's story by the chapter we just walked in on, no matter how it appears at the moment you entered.

In reading Proverbs 31, my natural tendency was to focus on the virtuous woman's perfection, so much so, that I failed to consider she, too, may have experienced some pain in her past. We don't know what someone has been through and, sometimes, we forget that God is ready to forgive our mistakes and transform us into the women He has called us to be. When God transforms us, He can use us in the church, our homes, our businesses, in government, and the world to make a difference. So, if God can forgive us, then forgive yourself for what you had to do while in survival mode. Be transformed; be who He has called you to be!

The Road to Virtue

Who am I talking to today? You may be a virtuous woman now, but nobody knows what you had to do in your past to stay alive. Maybe you've made decisions that weren't always the best or most popular, but you did what you had to do. You might be a corporate employee now, but there were some unsavory places you were forced to work just to survive.

Perhaps you entered into some relationships, against the advice of a friend or loved one, just so you could keep food in your baby's mouth. You aren't proud of it, and you would change it if you could, but you did what you thought you had to do to survive.

And, I believe Bathsheba could best advise her son about the virtuous woman because she knew what it was to be considered the alternative. Like most mothers, she wanted better for him. Even with her background, Bathsheba ultimately became a virtuous woman. She was the wife of the king, mother to the heir. But she didn't start off like that; she had a story.

And like Bathsheba, well-known women of today also have a story. For instance, she's Oprah now, but she was born into poverty in rural Mississippi to a teenage single mother, was abused sexually as a child, and became pregnant at fourteen.[17] She's Tina Turner now, but she was Anna Mae Bullock from Nutbush, Tennessee. She's Michelle Obama now, but she was Chelly from Chicago's south side.[18] She's JLo now—but, as she admits—don't be fooled by her rocks because she's still Jenny from around the block.

We had a past before we arrived at the place we're at now. That is why we shouldn't make rushed judgments or judge a woman based on what we see now. Every virtuous woman has a story, but we may not know the hard work and lessons they learned to get to where they are today.

You Are Not Alone

Proverbs 31 seems to paint the virtuous woman as a superwoman, but if we read closely, this isn't entirely the case at all: "She riseth also while it is yet night, and giveth meat to her household, and a portion to her maidens" (Proverbs 31:15 KJV).

When you read this verse, it's easy to believe she does all this by herself. If you're not careful, this part of her description is easy to overlook because it's just two words, but these two words make a big difference. You see, the reason the virtuous woman can accomplish all she does is that she had help from "her maidens." Likewise, we can't do life on our own. We need support from others.

In her book *Year of Yes*, Shonda Rhimes says:[19]

> You devote a chapter to your nanny, and you thank the five other members of your household staff. Why are working women ashamed to acknowledge that they have help? People don't want to acknowledge it. The people who work in my home were there at different times during the writing of the book. It's because you feel like— isn't that funny? I literally just did it! I just said, "I don't have five people..."

No one wants to admit they have help. So you see, if it weren't for Shonda Rhimes' help, we would not be able to enjoy *Grey's Anatomy* or *Scandal*. The Bible indicates this woman has maidens, women who serve her and help her when needed. This word *maiden* also translates to "girl" (Proverbs 31:15 NLT). So, when we say her maidens, we're also saying "her girls." So, you see, when she rises early in the morning and leaves the house, she can do so because one of her girls is watching the kids.

To be a virtuous woman, you need support. And what's interesting is that Solomon has a lot to say about support. In this same book of proverbs as good and bad character, support and friendship are highlighted multiple times.

> Oil and perfume make the heart glad, so a man's counsel is sweet to his friend.
> —***Proverbs 27:9***(NASB)

> A friend loves at all times, and a brother is born for adversity.
> —***Proverbs 17:17***(NASB)

And Solomon doesn't stop there. In the book of Ecclesiastes 4:9–12 (NIV), He continues to highlight the importance of a solid support system:

> Two are better than one, because they have a good return for their labor: If either of them falls down, one can help the other up. But pity anyone who falls and has no one to help them up. Also, if two lie down together, they will keep warm. But how can one keep warm alone? Though one may be overpowered, two can defend themselves. A cord of three strands is not quickly broken.

You can be a virtuous woman all you want, but don't think you're going to do it by your lonesome. Every woman needs some support! I, Rev. Tish, didn't get to be Rev. Tish without women like my mother, sister, aunts, and best friends who encouraged me and supported me.

You can do so much more in life when you have help

from your friends and family. And you ought to have different people for different things. I have friends I pray with, laugh with, cry with, and shop with (these are my favorite because they always encourage me to buy both pairs of shoes). And I have friends who keep some money or mints in their purse just in case. I think it takes a village to raise us, and I thank God for the village He gave me!

The Struggle Is Real

Let's face it; being a virtuous woman is a struggle sometimes! Despite what Proverbs 31:25 says—"Strength and honour are her clothing; and she shall rejoice in time to come" (KJV)—being busy 24/7 is exhausting. We must consider that while everything this woman does is impressive, she never stops. Her work is never-ending. The Bible never gives any indication of her having rest. She's up early and comes back home late. She constantly works—and that has got to be a struggle.

Do you feel like you're constantly working? It is easy to feel this real struggle. You're up early and home late. You're working full time or going to school, trying to raise your kids, in some cases alone. You sleep for a little while and wonder how you'll get the strength to do it all over again the next day.

And somehow, this woman, this virtuous superwoman, manages it all and does so with a positive attitude. How do I know? Because the Bible says that "strength and honor are her clothing and she shall rejoice in time to come." What does that mean? It means she endures the struggle because she knows a better day is coming.

Your time is coming! You may struggle with your classes now, but you know that degree is coming. You may struggle with the entry-level job, but a promotion is coming. And you may struggle "to make a dollar out of fifteen cents," but a wage increase is coming. Yes, the struggle is real, but we can rest in remembering that a new day is coming. What if it's hard because we feel like people can't see our struggle? If others could see our struggle, if they just knew our pain, then maybe it would be easier. Often, that is the case. Others fail to see our struggles.

If we look at the virtuous woman, all we see is what she has done and accomplished, and we don't see her while she's doing all those things. She makes everything she does look easy, but if I had to guess, I bet things were not as easy for her as they read in Proverbs 31. You don't make clothes without pricks from a needle. You don't get up while it's dark without clearing the crust from your eyes. You don't prepare food for your family without burning it occasionally. You don't work in the field without stepping in some mess. Yet those are definitely not the parts we see in Proverbs 31. We know she must do these things, but we never see how.

You see, as women, we have a way of making the difficult look easy. Just because you can juggle work, school, and family doesn't mean it's ever easy. Just because you can handle the kids, doesn't mean it's easy. Just because you're the caregiver and not the patient doesn't mean it's easy.

And because it looks so easy, we think no one sees our struggle. But be encouraged, because someone does see your struggle. In this case, the Bible says her family sees her struggle, and they praise her for it. Proverbs 31:28 says, "Her children arise up, and call her blessed; her husband also, and he praiseth her" (KJV). In her children and her husband praising her, I'm sure that helped to alleviate some of her stress and, perhaps, they helped her out occasionally.

Remember, no woman ever started a fight with her husband while he was doing the dishes. And just know that even if no one sees your struggle, God sees your struggle, and He will give you strength! Didn't He say that "those who hope in the LORD will renew their strength" (Isaiah 40:31 NIV)?

Strength for the Journey

A virtuous woman is a strong woman. When we hear the word virtuous, we automatically think of gracious, pious, or holier than thou. But it doesn't mean any of those things. What it really means is strength. It is strength to do what you need to do, to say what needs to be said, and to know what not to say. The virtuous woman is a strong woman. She isn't a shrinking violet afraid of confrontation. The Bible says the virtuous woman "girds herself with strength, and strengthens her arms" (Proverbs 31:17 NKJV). That means she's ready for battle! She faces life head-on with the strength and courage of a soldier despite the obstacles, the setbacks, the hardships, and the pain.

It takes strength to be a virtuous woman. Perhaps you have taken life's best shot and are still standing. Perhaps you are facing your greatest challenges yet, and still, have smiles on your faces. Maybe you have confronted the enemy and lived to tell the story. I see some women who are the head and not the tail (Deuteronomy 28:13), more than overcomers (Romans 8:37), walking in their authority.

But we don't do this on our own. Like the virtuous woman, your strength comes from God: "Charm is deceptive, and beauty is fleeting; but a woman who fears the LORD is to be praised" (Proverbs 31:30 NIV).

What does it mean to fear the Lord? It means the virtuous woman has enough respect for God to live a life that is pleasing to Him. When you're faithful to God, He is faithful to you. And He will give you the strength to endure, not so you can be Superwoman, but that you can be a strong, virtuous woman.

Should we strive to be the strong, virtuous woman? Yes, we should. Will we miss the mark of perfection sometimes? Yes, we will. Should that stop us? No, of course not. You may not be perfect, but God can use you to achieve His perfect will, even though we women are far from perfect.

When you look at Matthew 1 and consider Jesus' lineage, you may notice the women listed were far from perfect, and yet, God used them. Bathsheba—we already know her story. Rahab was a known prostitute. Tamar was wronged by her father-in-law, half-brother, and multiple husbands. And let's not forget Mary, an unwed, pregnant, teenaged mother from Galilee. They, or their lives, may not have been perfect, but they brought about God's perfect will—Jesus.

You may not be a superwoman, but you are God's woman. You may never be perfect because you may be weak. But that's okay because, in your weakness, God is made perfect (2 Corinthians 12:9).

You may never be perfect because you're too meek. Don't worry—Jesus said the meek will inherit the earth (Matthew 5:5). Or, you may never be perfect because you're too bold, but you can continue boldly before the throne of grace (Hebrews 4:16 KJV).

You may never be perfect because you're too salty. That's okay; you can be the salt of the earth (Matthew 5:13)! You may never be perfect because you're weird, but you can be weird in a way that pleases God, who says we are a peculiar people (1 Peter 2:9 KJV).

Perhaps you'll never be perfect because you talk too much. Well, talk to Jesus and "pray continually" (1 Thessalonians 5:17 NIV). You may never be a perfect leader, and maybe sometimes nobody will follow you—but if you lean on God, goodness, and mercy will follow you all the days of your life (Psalm 23:6)!

You may not feel perfect because of your age, but Scripture encourages us, "Don't let anyone look down on you because you are young, but set an example for the believers in speech, in conduct, in love, in faith and in purity" (1 Timothy 4:12 NIV). Young or old, you can model Jesus' love to others!

You may not be perfect because trials have worn you down to the point that you and your life feel boring and bland. But even if you've lost your zest for life, God encourages you to "taste and see that the LORD is good" (Psalm 34:8 NRSV).

You may not be able to succeed or persevere perfectly amid difficult circumstances, but you can do all things through Christ, who strengthens you (Philippians 4:13). And no, your situation won't always be perfect, but God is ready to work things out for your good (Romans 8:28).

God can use you now, just as you are, on your journey to becoming virtuous. You might see yourself as a failure, but God's strength is made perfect in your weakness, and He can use your mistakes for His good purposes. You're not a superwoman, but you're God's woman!

You Are God's Woman

You May Feel Too:	But God Says:
Weak	In your weakness, His strength is perfect. (2 Corinthians 12:9–10)
Meek	The meek will inherit the earth. (Matthew 5:5)
Helpless and frustrated	All things will work together for your good. (Romans 8:28–29)
Bold	Come boldly before the throne of grace. (Hebrews 4:16)
Salty	You are the salt of the earth. (Matthew 5:13)
Talkative	Pray continually. (1 Thessalonians 5:17)
Unable to get others to follow you	Goodness and mercy will follow you all the days of your life. (Psalm 23:6)
Weird	You are a "peculiar" people. (1 Peter 2:9)
Young (or old)	You will see God's faithfulness all your days. (Psalm 37:25)
Bland and worn out	Taste and see that the Lord is good. (Psalm 34:8)
Unable to persevere or succeed	You can do all things through Christ. (Philippians 4:13)

WORKBOOK

Chapter Three Questions

Question: What are your impressions of the Proverbs 31 woman? Do you see her as an ideal to aspire to, or as an impossible pinnacle to obtain? Read through this chapter with grace lenses, thinking of the flawed women in Jesus' own genealogy—and in your life—and how these qualities might apply to women in many different life circumstances.

_____
_____
_____
_____
_____
_____
_____
_____

Question: How might the mistakes and struggles of your past motivate you to become a better woman—a virtuous woman—today?

_____
_____
_____
_____
_____
_____
_____
_____
_____
_____

Question: The virtuous woman had her maidens to help her accomplish so much. Do you willingly ask for help when you need it, or do you try to go it alone? Who are the friends/relatives/church family/etc. who are your support system? If you do not have such a network, why not? What can you do to start building one now?

_____
_____
_____
_____
_____

_____

_____

_____

_____

_____

_____

_____

Journal: What is some life advice your mother gave you that has shaped you over the years? If you could summarize everything you want to pass on to your children (or those younger in your sphere of influence if you don't have children) into a few paragraphs, what would you tell them?

Action: Who is a woman you know who makes the difficult look easy? Who maintains a positive attitude in her struggles that a better day is coming? Who exudes strength in and through the Lord's strength? Write her a note or send her a message this week to thank her for being a model of a virtuous woman in your life.

Chapter Three Notes

CHAPTER FOUR

Who Is She?

I beseech Euodias, and beseech Syntyche, that they be of the same mind in the Lord.

And I intreat thee also, true yokefellow, help those women which laboured with me in the gospel, with Clement also, and with other my fellow labourers, whose names are in the book of life.

—*Philippians 4:2-3*(KJV)

The Bible has a lot to say about conflict. It begins in the Garden of Eden (Genesis 3) and continues throughout. The following timeless illustration shows the age-old issue of conflict in an interesting way.

In a sermon given by David Daniels, he tells a story of a couple who had been married for sixty years:[20]

> ...throughout their life, they had shared everything. They loved each other deeply. They had not kept any secrets from one another, except for a small shoe box that the wife kept in the top shelf of her closet. When they got married, she put the box there and asked her husband never to look inside of it and never to ask questions about its contents.

For sixty years, the man honored his wife's request. In fact, he forgot about the box until a day when his wife grew gravely ill, and the doctors were sure she had no way of recovering. So the man, putting his wife's affairs into order, remembered that box in the top of her closet, got it down, and brought it to her at the hospital. He asked her if perhaps now they might be able to open it. She agreed. They opened the box, and inside were two crocheted dolls and a roll of money that totaled $95,000. The man was astonished.

The woman told her husband that the day before they were married, her grandmother told her that if she and her husband were ever to get into an argument with one another, they should work hard to reconcile, and if they were unable to reconcile, she should simply keep her mouth shut and crochet a doll. The man was touched by this because there were only two crocheted dolls in the box. He was amazed that over sixty years of marriage, they apparently had had only two conversations that they were unable to reconcile. Tears came to his eyes, and he grew even more deeply in love with this woman. Then he asked about the roll of money. "What's with this?" he asked. His wife said, "Well, every time I crocheted a doll, I sold it to a local craft fair for five dollars."

I am sure this husband must have been shocked to find his wife had been upset with him that much.

But the reality is, it is impossible to be in a marriage, on a job, in our family, in a relationship, or even in a church without experiencing some kind of conflict with someone. While conflict isn't a bad thing, it needs to be handled well to be beneficial for the people involved.

On the flip side, you can even have conflict within yourself. Eat the cake; don't eat the cake. Buy the shoes; don't buy the shoes. Go to the gym; don't go to the gym.

Conflict is unavoidable in any instance, whether it be with people or with us. Throughout the Bible, there is no shortage of people who experienced conflict. Choose any example, and you will find that conflict was always present in their lives. Deborah, Naomi, Mary, and even Jesus all experienced conflict. And if that's not enough, even in the most perfect place ever created, the Garden of Eden, conflict was present.

In short, conflict is unavoidable no matter who you are or where you are. The dictionary definition for *conflict* is "to come into collision or disagreement; be contradictory ... or in opposition."[21]

Sounds bad, doesn't it? However, despite how bad conflict may sound, conflict is not a bad thing and it has its benefits. Without conflict, there would never be a good book to read. Without conflict, you would never tune in to your favorite television show. Without conflict, no new ideas would ever be created. Without conflict, you would never be able to see another perspective. And believe it or not, without conflict, you would never learn new things about yourself.

Conflict is not a bad thing in and of itself. However, you must know how to handle it. In the Bible, we see a classic example of a conflict between two women, and how the apostle Paul handles it.

Who Were Euodia and Syntyche?

Here Paul introduced us to two women in the church of Philippi who were involved in a conflict tangle of some sort, and he requested that they be of the same mind. However, this lesson is not about two women but rather people in general because there are a Euodia and a Syntyche in every church.

Let me explain who these women are. First, Paul says, these two women "labored with [him] in the gospel" (Philippians 4:3 NKJV). An article entitled "Women Leaders in the Philippian Church" offers valuable insight into who these women were:[22]

> When he describes the ministry of Euodia and Syntyche, Paul uses some of the same terms he had previously applied to Timothy and Epaphroditus. Paul writes that Euodia and Syntyche had contended with him "in the gospel." Earlier in the same letter, Paul had also described Timothy as someone who had served with him "in the gospel" (Philippians 2:22). Paul goes on to refer to Euodia and Syntyche as his "co-workers." Earlier, Paul had also referred to Epaphroditus as his "co-worker" (Philippians 2:25 NIV). Thus, according to Paul, the ministries of these women were comparable to the ministries of the men, Timothy and Epaphroditus.

This tells us that for all intents and purposes, these women were preachers, and they both shared the gospel. They were both on the Lord's team doing His work. But, unfortunately, they experienced conflict. This indicates that preachers are not immune from conflict and can experience one with other preachers or even their congregation.

Although we aren't clear about the role of Euodia and Syntyche in the early church, it is possible they were the leaders of the Philippian church with multiples responsibilities for running the business of the church. In short, they may have been trustees, and like modern trustees would have been susceptible to conflict.

What's interesting to note is Paul never indicates what the conflict is about. We have no idea what these two people disagreed with.

Perhaps Euodia and Syntyche disagreed for many of the same reasons we do in the church today. Perhaps, Euodia came into the service that day and found Syntyche in her seat. Maybe it was Euodia's turn to pray, and Syntyche found herself doing it—again. Or maybe, the church anniversary was approaching, and they couldn't agree on the napkin or plate colors.

Could it be that Syntyche was the choir director, and

Euodia was upset because she had to sing that song one more time? Maybe Syntyche didn't sell her raffle tickets and now they missed the goal. It's possible Euodia missed praise dance rehearsal but showed up dressed and ready to go on Sunday.

We don't know what caused the conflict between these two women. But we do know they had two very distinct personalities. In biblical times, names always had meaning behind them and were always very indicative of one's personality or main character trait.

The name Euodia comes from the Greek verb *euodoo*,[23] which means "to grant a prosperous and expeditious journey."[24] In other words, *euodoo* indicates movement and is synonymous with the phrase "bon voyage." Perhaps Euodia was likely in a constant state of movement, always ready for progression—always ready for the next step, to take it to the next level.

The name Syntyche, on the other hand, comes from the Greek word *suntuchia*,[25] which means "the unexpected coinciding of two events, happening by chance"[26] In other words, her name meant serendipity or a happy accident. She was likely more laid back, relying on fate, and was content to wait and see what happened.

It's no wonder these two were in conflict. Where one was focused and goal-oriented, the other was happy to ride the wave and let the chips fall where they may. And now, the women who contended at Paul's side are now contending with each other.

Now, we don't know everything about the Philippian church, but based on the love Paul had for its members, the support they gave him, and that they were considered a model church, we know this church was growing—converting people left and right, seats were running over. I can imagine the spirit of the church was always at an all-time high! And maybe Euodia was ready to grow with it, while Syntyche was content just to see what happened.

We don't know what the conflict was between Euodia and Syntyche, but people inside and outside our churches experience that very same conflict today!

And, since we don't know what the particular conflict between these two women was about, the Scripture shows us Paul doesn't address the *conflict*, but rather addresses the women involved. We learn it doesn't matter what the conflict is, but *how* we handle it does matter.

Handling Conflict the Christian Way

Paul teaches us several important things about conflict. Conflict can't be covered up. Conflict must be handled with care. Conflict requires collaboration, and we must remember we're Christian.

When we consider the book of Philippians, the last thing we think of is conflict. Why? Because this is Paul's love letter to the church, this is his thank you letter for all the support they have shown. Many say Philippians is Paul's joy letter, so there should not be any conflict within, as the overall tone of the book is one of encouragement.

When you think about it, we may quote the book of Philippians more than any other book of the Bible. We see and say such things as "Rejoice in the Lord always: and again I say, Rejoice" (4:4 KJV); "And my God will supply all your needs according to His riches in glory in Christ Jesus" (4:19 NASB); "I have learned to be content" (4:11 NASB); "I press toward the mark for the prize of the high calling of God in Christ Jesus" (3:14 KJV); and "I can do all things through Christ who strengthens me" (4:13 NKJV).

Surprisingly, in the midst of all of the joy in this letter from Paul, there is a touch of pain between two people. And though we may want to focus on all the joyful things, we can't gloss over the conflict of what was happening.

That's because conflict can't be covered up, and it's virtually impossible for people to move on.

It's important to notice that right in the middle of his letter, Paul stops abruptly to address these two people. He must have felt this was too important to act like it wasn't important or pretend it didn't exist.

And I think that's because Paul knew more than anyone the impact that conflict could have on church leaders and, ultimately, the church as a whole. If you go back to Acts 15:36–41, you'll find Paul and Barnabas had experienced some clashes of their own.

Paul and Barnabas were about to embark on their second journey to visit the churches of Asia Minor (Turkey). Barnabas wanted to bring John Mark, who had started out with them on their first journey but had bailed out shortly after the trip began. Paul was adamant that John Mark should not go with them. Acts 15:39 says, "They had such a sharp disagreement that they parted company" (NIV). Barnabas took John Mark and sailed to Cyprus, and Paul took Silas and went north through Syria and Cilicia.

Separating from a church, relationship, or job is not always pleasant, especially when it is a result of conflict. It was no different for Paul—because they had been through a lot together, this must have been painful for them both. Even though their conflict was a serious struggle, they continued to preach the gospel, allowing God to use them. Instead of one mission team, there were now two, and so the message of Jesus was preached in places never heard before.

Although not every conflict has a positive result, it's important to seek understanding and peace when conflict arises. This was something Paul understood, so before he continued, he spoke of the peace that defies understanding as he dealt with this situation (Philippians 4:7). He knew unless you deal with the conflict, there can be no peace.

Covering a Conflict Makes Things Worse

Paul didn't cover up the conflict; he exposed it. Many believe that covering up the conflict will make it go away. On the contrary, covering up conflict only makes things worse. It's like a child who gets a cut, and all they want you to do is put a Band-Aid on it. They don't want to clean the cut; they want to cover it and pretend it isn't there. But the infection is still there and can spread if it is covered too long. Sometimes the best thing to do is expose the cut even if it hurts a bit, so you can clean it out.

And that's what happens when a conflict between people is covered up. The relationship might look nice and neat on the outside, but soon unresolved feelings, resentment, and negative emotions get in like germs, and soon you have a conflict infection that spreads.

That was Paul's fear with these church leaders, Euodia and Syntyche. If the conflict between them was not nipped in the bud, if it wasn't cleaned up immediately, this conflict between them had the potential to spread and infect the whole church.

Why? Because without being cleaned out, nasty, infectious things like gossip and speculation get in, and before you know it, a small cut becomes so infected that it's a major problem. Paul was trying to avoid potential major problems when he called out Euodia and Syntyche by name.

Paul's intention in addressing the conflict between Euodia and Syntyche wasn't to shame them but to encourage them to patch things up. Because he loved them, his intention was never to hurt but to heal.

Consider your children when they do something wrong. When you discipline them, it's never to hurt them but to help them and prevent the behavior from happening in the future. It's called discipline.

When we fail to correct the wrong, it's as if we foresee

happening to us what happened with David and his children in the Old Testament. David avoided the conflict with his son Absalom and failed to discipline Amnon (2 Samuel 13–15). When David finally decided to deal with his sons, Amnon was dead, and Absalom hated David so much he conspired to take over the kingdom. We learn from these biblical examples that love requires discipline!

When you love someone, you correct them. When you love someone, you pull their coattails. When you love someone, it's ok to correct them because the Bible tells me that even God "disciplines those he loves" (Hebrews 12:6 NLT).

Fragile—Handle with Care

Paul decided to uncover the conflict between these two women because he loved them, and he loved the church. When he addressed them, he did so with care. All conflict must be handled with care. We see how Paul entreated both of these women because he besought them, as Philippians 4:2 (KJV) says, "I beseech Euodias, and beseech Syntyche." Paul was careful in his approach and his words.

If you've ever packed boxes before moving or sent out a package with fragile contents, then you are familiar with the expression "handle with care." This phrase indicates to the carrier that what's inside is extremely fragile, and if it's not handled with great care, then everything inside could get broken.

Well, like a fragile package, there are some delicate things wrapped up in conflict—things that can be easily broken if not handled with care: feelings, egos, friendships, relationships, and reputations are wrapped in conflict.

And when you don't handle it with care, when you open it, everything inside is a broken mess. It is evident by the way Paul addresses these two that he understands the fragility of the situation. Fragility isn't always negative. In fact, it is paramount to understanding the wound and the depth of the pain that could be there, and therefore being careful with the person's feelings, as a doctor would when tending to a physical injury. We must be delicate in our tone when handling conflict.

The Tone Sets the Tone

Notice the tone Paul uses in dealing with these two women. He says, "I beseech Euodias, and beseech Syntyche." *Beseech* means "to beg anxiously."[27] He was literally begging them, imploring them to fix things. Notice he didn't request, he didn't demand, but he begged them.

And Paul was smart. He didn't add fuel to the fire by using the wrong tone. And that's where we mess up. He wasn't accusatory or argumentative. He knew the situation was already volatile.

The last thing you want to do in a hostile situation is to use the wrong tone. Often, it's our tone, not the specific words we say, that frames our communication.

The right tone can keep you from getting a parking ticket. The right tone can get a scared animal to eat from your hand. The right tone can prevent a suicide. The right tone can set hostages free.

Married people really understand the importance of tone. You can tell by the way your spouse addresses you what kind of conversation it's going to be. If they call you by your pet name, "Hey, sweetie," then you know all is right with the world, and it's going to be a good day for everybody. If they address you by your everyday term of endearment like "babe" or "honey," then it's no big deal; maybe they just need to know where you put the car keys. But you know something is up, and it's about to go down, when they call you by your full name.

So as we see in our personal relationships, our tone is very important when it comes to resolving conflict. You can't approach people yelling, screaming, and making demands. If you do, you can expect the same behavior toward you.

The wrong tone, the one with bass in it, is when what could have been a manageable conflict turns into a full fight or battle. That is, the tone of voice of the parties indicates neither party wants to resolve conflict or seek to understand the emotions behind the conflict any longer. They have resolved to handle it by less effective means.

Like Paul's, your tone should be indicative of wanting to solve the problem, not make it bigger. When conflict arises, set the tone for the first meeting by saying something like: "I want us to come to an agreement on this," or "I believe we can work together to resolve this problem."

In conflict or out of conflict, we should always speak to each other in love, especially as Christians. You can say anything to anyone if you say it in love. We can say anything in love because the Bible says we can. First Corinthians 13:1 illustrates that "If I speak in the tongues of men and of angels, but have not love, I am a noisy gong or a clanging cymbal" (ESV). In other words, you can say all the right things, but they won't mean anything if it is not motivated by love. And the key to resolving conflict is the power between the wrong tone or the right tone.

Paul wasn't expecting Euodias and Syntyche to solve this problem on their own. He expected the other leaders to get involved as well because sometimes solving conflict takes collaboration.

The Conflict Is Not Yours Alone

Ministry is a team effort. And when one person on the

team hurts, we all hurt. And when conflict hurts one faction of the church, it hurts the whole church. That is why Paul says, "And I intreat thee also, true yokefellow, help those women" (Philippians 4:3 KJV).

What is important to note is Paul does not encourage the other leaders to take sides. He says, "Help those women." The natural inclination in any conflict is to want to pick a side. Paul didn't say make sure Syntyche apologizes. He didn't ask the church to help Euodias see the error of her ways. But rather he said to help *both* of them. Because in the end, it doesn't matter who's right or who's wrong. All that matters is the situation is resolved.

Sometimes in the midst of conflict, the people involved don't always see things clearly. When tempers flare, and emotions run high, it becomes very difficult to think rationally or even see the situation objectively enough to want to make things right. That is why it is the responsibility of the other believers or "yokefellow"—those united by a bond—to help resolve things.

How do I know helping each other to resolve conflict is our responsibility? Again, because of Paul's tone. While he beseeches or lovingly begs the two women—he *entreats* the "true yokefellows."

To entreat also means to beg, but it's more of a request, which means "I'm begging you, and I expect it to be done." Let me help you. Another time the word *entreat* is used in the Bible is when Moses asked Pharaoh when he should "entreat [God] for [him]" (Exodus 8:9 NASB) meaning, "I'll beg God to do it and it will be done."

So, you see, when Paul entreated the "true yokefellows," he wasn't saying they *should* help resolve this conflict, he was saying you *must* help resolve this conflict! Notice, however, Paul said, I'm entreating the "true yokefellows" or the true Christians. *True,* in this context, means those Christians who are "loyal, legitimate, or genuine."[28]

The fact that Paul had to specify tells us there must have been some *false* yokefellows.

This example of a false yokefellow reminds me of those all-out school fights after school back in the day. When I was in school, there was always the promise of a fight at 3:00 p. m. All the kids would gather around, waiting for the main event, and then create a circle around the fighters. I remember the fighters would go around in their own circle forever, talking to each other and never throwing a punch.

But there was always that one person in the crowd who would shove one of the fighters toward the other fighter to make it appear as though the first punch was thrown, thereby setting it off. That's what you call a false yokefellow, someone who has the potential to stop the fight but chooses to keep it going instead.

There's always going to be someone to stir the pot. There's always going to be someone who keeps the gossip going. There's always going to be someone who loves the drama. There's always going to be someone to fan the flame.

But, I thank God for the true yokefellows because, although there is one person who is there to start the fight, there is always one person there to break up the fight.

A true yokefellow says, "Hey! It's not worth it." A true yokefellow mediates and doesn't aggravate. A true yokefellow stops the fight before it even gets started! A true yokefellow knows if the fighters get in trouble, everybody gets in trouble because the fellowship and friendship have been broken.

True yokefellows—that's who Paul was talking to. And I don't know about you, but I want to be a true yokefellow because the Bible says, "Blessed are the peacemakers, for they shall be called sons of God" (Matthew 5:9 NKJV). And when we are acting in peace, we are in the Lord.

Being "In the Lord"

To be a Christian means to "be of the same mind in the Lord" (Philippians 4:2 NIV). As Christians, we may not be able to agree on much. But here's one thing I'm sure we can all agree on: we all love the Lord. There is a saying, "Talk about *what* you believe and you have disunity. Talk about *who* you believe in and you have unity."[29]

I talked a lot about what we don't know when it comes to these two women, Euodias and Syntyche. We don't know what the conflict was about, and we don't know who's right and who's wrong. We don't know when the conflict started or even if they resolved it.

But here's what we do know: they loved God. They were leaders in the church. They believed in the gospel of Jesus Christ. Someone among them was a true yokefellow, and their names are written in the Book of Life. In other words, they were in the Lord! And when you're in the Lord, it means you're a Christian. And when conflict arises, it means you have to handle it as such.

I believe Paul saw the potential for danger here, which is why he encouraged Euodias and Syntyche to be of the same mind "In the Lord." Even though they were both working for the Lord, I'm sure up until this point, they were trying to do things in themselves. And when we do things in ourselves, we can't be in the Lord very well. These women were to solve their disagreement, not in their own way, but in and through Christ—then, and only then, would they be effective in the Lord.

I don't know about you, but when I try to do things without the Lord, it doesn't always work out for me. But Paul uses the phrase "*in* the Lord." Paul saw the potential problem here. You may not want to admit it, but when I think about conflict and some I have had over the years, I remember how dangerous it can be to handle things without the Lord, and I wish I had a Paul to remind me to stay *in* the Lord.

If I "stay in the Tisha," someone could get hurt. As a matter of fact, we have the potential to stay everywhere except in the Lord when conflict arises. We stay in hurt; we stay in the anger, we stay in pain, we stay in the frustration—we stay in our feelings.

I challenge you to stay in the Lord because there is no better place to be than in the Lord. Stay safe *in* His arms. There's safety *in* His house (Proverbs 18:10), humility *in* His presence (James 4:10), the whole world is *in* His hands (Psalm 95:4). We can enter *into* His gates with thanksgiving (Psalm 100:4), enter *into* His courts with praise because you were made *in* His image (Genesis 1:27), and you are precious *in* His sight (Isaiah 43:4).

Stay *in* the Lord because something very special happens. When you stay *in* the Lord, the Lord will stay *in* you! How do I know? Because He said it: "For where two or three are gathered together *in* My name, I am there *in* the midst of them" (Matthew 18:20 NKJV). And, "if you remain *in* me and I *in* you, you will bear much fruit" (John 15:5 NIV). I can ask what I will, *in* His name (John 14:13). We will abide *in* Him and He *in* us, because He has given us His Spirit, as He promised, "the Spirit who lives *in* you is greater than the spirit who lives *in* the world" (1 John 4:4 NLT).

When it comes to conflict, you can forget who you are. Paul reminds us we need to focus on whose we are! This is why Paul specified they be of the *same* mind in the Lord.

When you get into conflict, it's very easy to lose sight of what's important. Paul reminded them they were laborers in the gospel, and more importantly, their names were in the Book of Life.

Euodias and Syntyche were focused on this conflict when they needed to be focused on the work of the Lord.

The work of the Lord is far more important than any conflict you have going on. Unless you get things right with your brother, you can't do anything for God. You can't give your mind, your time, or your energy because all those things get consumed in fueling the problems and conflict. And as if that's not bad enough, you can't even give God your gifts. Jesus said, "Leave your gift there before the altar and go. First be reconciled to your brother, and then come and offer your gift" (Matthew 5:24 ESV).

The enemy knows that if he can get your mind, he can keep it off the work that needs to be done. And when the work is not done, the whole church body suffers. Euodias and Syntyche needed to be on the same page, with one accord, and of the same mind so that the church could remain unified. Philippians 2:2 says to "fulfill my joy by being like-minded, having the same love, being of one accord, of one mind" (NKJV).

And to be of the same mind, someone has to humble themselves. Someone has to be willing to give up what it is they want for the greater good. Someone has to be willing to set aside the attitude; someone has to be willing to give up what they want to resolve the conflict.

Isn't that what Jesus did for us? Jesus not only did all that, but He also rose above the conflicts and overcame!

You Can Rise Above the Conflicts!

I'm reminded of the time I visited Rome. The architecture is amazing. There are fountains, ruins, and all sorts of buildings and temples. Every single one of them means something, and each one tells a story.

Near one main area is a column featuring the Roman emperor Marcus Aurelius. On this huge, tall column are carved images that tell the story of a war and conflict Aurelius had.

Our tour guide explained that on the top of the column,

interestingly, stands not Marcus Aurelius, but the apostle Paul. This might seem strange to have Marcus Aurelius and the apostle Paul on the same statue, but once Christianity became legal, all pagan and imperial images were destroyed and replaced with Christian ones.

So in a sense, the apostle Paul is standing on top of all this war and bloodshed, reminding us that Christians can always rise above the conflict.

The tour guide also shared that not only was Paul on top of the column but he was also strategically positioned to look out over Rome as though looking toward the future. This reveals to us that to overcome conflict as Christians; we must look toward the future.

There is "stuff" that has happened to you. There are wars that have given you the reminders of battle wounds that signify your struggle. But, you don't have to stay in the struggle, in the hurt, or in the pain. You can get through it. Rise! Put all that conflict under your feet and use it as the stepping stone to your future.

Yes, we have to stay in the Lord, but if you find yourself staying instead in conflict, let me tell you about a Savior who I love who can pull you out. His name is Jesus.

Jesus is a master at resolving conflict. When your body's in conflict, He heals you. When your mind is in conflict, He regulates it. When your home is in conflict, He gives you peace.

It's like Philippians 2:5–11 (NKJV) tells us:

> Let this mind be in you which was also in Christ Jesus, who, being in the form of God, did not consider it robbery to be equal with God, but made Himself of no reputation, taking the form of a bondservant, and coming in the likeness of men. And being found in appearance as a man, He humbled Himself and became obedient to the point of death, even the death of the cross. Therefore God also has highly exalted Him and given Him the name which is above every

name, that at the name of Jesus every knee should bow, of those in heaven, and of those on earth, and of those under the earth, and that every tongue should confess that Jesus Christ is Lord, to the glory of God the Father.

Christ beseeches us to resolve our conflict and be in Him just as Paul beseeched Euodias and Syntyche to resolve their conflict. It should be our desire, as Christians, to live a life of peace so we can endeavor to please the Lord, who has given us salvation.

To further illustrate this point of clearing up conflict between your fellow Christian friend, let me share another story that I think emphasizes the point:[30]

> There was once an old stone monastery tucked away in the middle of a picturesque forest. For many years people would make the significant detour required to see out this monastery. The peaceful spirit of the place was healing the soul.
>
> In recent years, however, fewer and fewer people were making their way to the monastery. The monks had grown jealous and petty in their relationships with one another, and the animosity was felt by those who visited.
>
> The Abbot of the monastery was distressed by what was happening, and poured out his heart to his good friend Jeremiah. Jeremiah was a wise old Jewish rabbi. Having heard the Abbot's tale of woe he asked if he could offer a suggestion. "Please do," responded the Abbot. "Anything you can offer."
>
> Jeremiah said that he had received a vision, an important vision, and the vision was this: the messiah was among the ranks of the monks. The Abbot was flabbergasted. One among his own was the Messiah! Who could it be? He knew it wasn't himself, but who? He raced back to the monastery and shared his exciting news with his fellow monks.

The monks grew silent as they looked into each other's faces. Was this one the Messiah?

From that day on, the mood in the monastery changed. Joseph and Ivan started talking again, neither wanting to be guilty of slighting the Messiah. Pierre and Naibu left behind their frosty anger and sought out each other's forgiveness. The monks began serving each other, looking out for opportunities to assist, seeking healing and forgiveness where offence had been given.

As one traveler, then another, found their way to the monastery word soon spread about the remarkable spirit of the place. People once again took the journey to the monastery and found themselves renewed and transformed. All because those monks knew the Messiah was among them.

In this matter of shoring up conflict between others, we must live like Jesus is among us because He is! When we let conflict pile on top of us, we can't stand firm and do what God has called us to do because we're overwhelmed with the weight of everything we're carrying on our shoulders.

We must trust that God is right there in the conflict, working for our good and His glory as He urges us toward reconciliation and preserving the beautiful relationships with those around us.

WORKBOOK

Chapter Four Questions

Question: What are some conflicts in your life right now (note: these could involve family, church, work, friends, or the community)? Has your focus been on resolving the situation peacefully or has your focus been on how wrong the other party is and trying to make them change? What are some possible good things that could come from these conflicts?

_____

_____

_____

_____

_____

_____

_____

_____

Question: Is your usual response to cover up conflict or to expose it? What are the dangers of covering up conflict? What tone or attitude is essential for exposing and resolving it?

_____
_____
_____
_____
_____
_____
_____
_____
_____
_____

Question: Who is an objective, sincere someone who can help you find a peaceful resolution to the conflicts you face?

_____
_____
_____
_____
_____
_____

_____

_____

_____

_____

_____

Journal: Are you staying *in the Lord* or in "your feelings"—your frustration, your bitterness, your anger, etc.? How will you keep your focus on what is to come rather than what is behind, on the eternal rather than the temporal?

Action: Euodias's and Syntyche's unique personalities and perspectives probably contributed to their unnamed disagreement. Do a study on the different personality types and how they interact together. How can understanding others' personalities and your own help in conflict resolution?

Chapter Four Notes

CHAPTER FIVE

The Rahab Rehab

Then she let them down by a rope through the window, for her house was on the outer side of the city wall and she resided within the wall itself. She said to them, "Go toward the hill country, so that the pursuers may not come upon you. Hide yourselves there three days, until the pursuers have returned; then afterward you may go your way." The men said to her, "We will be released from this oath that you have made us swear to you if we invade the land and you do not tie this crimson cord in the window through which you let us down, and you do not gather into your house your father and mother, your brothers, and all your family. If any of you go out of the doors of your house into the street, they shall be responsible for their own death, and we shall be innocent; but if a hand is laid upon any who are with you in the house, we shall bear the responsibility for their death. But if you tell this business of ours, then we shall be released from this oath that you made us swear to you." She said, "According to your words, so be it." She sent them away and they departed. Then she tied the crimson cord in the window.
—*Joshua 2:15–21*(NRSV)

We often hear the prayer, "God grant me the serenity to accept the things I cannot change, courage to change the things I can, and wisdom to know the difference."[31]

This is commonly known as the Serenity Prayer. We all know the Serenity Prayer. You've seen it on coffee mugs, embossed on prayer journals, and bumper stickers. But, what you may not know is it doesn't stop there. The prayer continues:[32]

> *Living one day at a time; enjoying one moment at a time; accepting hardships as the pathway to peace; taking, as He did, this sinful world as it is, not as I would have it; trusting that He will make all things right if I surrender to His will; that I may be reasonably happy in this life and supremely happy with Him forever in the next. Amen.*

You also may not know that this prayer was composed in the 1930s by author Reinhold Niebuhr who used portions of the prayer in his sermons. Alcoholics Anonymous adopted the Serenity Prayer and began including it in their AA materials in 1942, which has done more to popularize this prayer than any message preached at church, any coffee mug, or tapestry display.[33]

Here, we find a prayer being made popular by those suffering from drug and alcohol abuse. Well, long before 1942, God has been using flawed concepts, ideas, and people to bring about order, glory, and His perfect will. And there is arguably no one who knew this better than Rahab—or as she is more famously known, Rahab, the prostitute.

God Wants to Associate with You!

Indeed, people who read the Bible are surprised to find a prostitute being praised as an example of faith, but in two separate places in the New Testament, the prostitute named Rahab is commended—she's listed as part of the lineage of Jesus in Matthew 1:5, and she's mentioned in the great Christians' Hall of Fame in Hebrews 11:31! Even though she had a sinful past, Rahab's great faith in the Lord gave her a significant role in Israelite history.

There are plenty of women in this world named Mary—everyone wants to be a woman of blessings and favor. There is no shortage of Elizabeths in this world—who doesn't want to be pious and God-fearing? You'll even find your fair share of Sarahs because who doesn't want to be beautiful and stunning? But you never hear of anyone naming their child Rahab because who wants to have a connection with the name of a prostitute?

Who, you ask, would want to associate with a prostitute? I can tell you who wants to be associated with a prostitute: God does (Matthew 21:31–32; Luke 15:1–2)!

I want to encourage you and let you know that no matter where you are, God wants to associate with you! If you're a drug addict, God wants to associate with you. If you're broken, God wants to associate with you. If you're guilt-ridden, wounded, or a hot mess, God wants to associate with you! And, even if you're angry with God, guess what? He still wants to associate with you!

Whatever condition you are in today, whatever people have called you, or whatever people have labeled you, let me encourage you by saying God still wants to associate with you!

God can and will use you. God can and will bless you. God can and will keep you, but, as the Serenity Prayer suggests and Rahab demonstrates, you have to surrender to Him!

But to do that, some of you will have to go to rehab. For some of us, rehab just sounds scary. But, there are actually several definitions of rehab that offer a sense of encouragement and hope.

Rehab is short for rehabilitation, which means "The action of restoring someone to health or normal life through training and therapy after imprisonment, addiction, or illness."[34]

You don't have to be in jail to be in prison. Some of us are trapped in the prisons of our minds, in a difficult relationship, or working a dead-end job.

You may not be on drugs or addicted to alcohol, but let's keep it one hundred percent, and admit that some of us have been addicted to situations, conditions, practices, and thought processes that are more dangerous than any narcotic. You may be: hooked on hatred, drunk with defeat, doped up on depression, lit by low self-esteem, wasted on *"why me?,"* inebriated with insecurities, or tied up by temptation.

It's not drugs, alcohol, sex, shopping, or gambling that's killing you; it's everything else! Rehabilitation can help us out of these traps, restore our relationship with God, and set us back in favor with Him.

Rehab is also "the action of restoring someone to former privileges or reputation after a period of disfavor."[35] Haven't we all fallen out of favor at some time in our lives? You're wifey one minute, then all of a sudden, the calls stop coming. You fell out of favor. Haven't we all lost a job or been demoted? You were the top executive, but now here's the new guy who seems to be rising to the top.

God is simply telling us, "Surrender to Me, and I'll restore the years the locusts have eaten. I'll show you favor!"

Rehab has another meaning, which is "the action of restoring something that has been damaged to its former condition."[36] Perhaps you experienced a nasty breakup, and you don't believe in love the way you used to. Maybe your trust was broken, and now you can't believe in people the way you used to. You were on top of the world, and you lost it just like that.

God tells us we shouldn't worry about the damage

that's been done because He is doing a new thing (Isaiah 43:19 NIV). And if you're reading this, then you know; He's already begun that work in you.

If any of these conditions apply to you, then consider this your intervention. It's time to go to rehab—but not just any rehab. You need the *Rahab Rehab*!

What Does Rahab Rehab Look Like?

Rahab realized that to change her life, her status, and her situation; she had to surrender to a power greater than herself and turn her life over to the care of God as she understood Him.

All most people know about Rahab is that she was a harlot, a prostitute. But she was more than that—she believed in God and was included in the lineage of Jesus Christ. God used her, though she was a broken woman, to do something great.

God has instructed Joshua, the newly minted leader of the people of Israel, to cross the Jordan and claim the land that God had given the Israelites (Joshua 1:9). And God promises Joshua that just as He was always with Moses, his predecessor, He will be with him as well.

And so Joshua, strong and courageous, proceeds to conquer the land, not knowing all the details of how God would keep this promise. Joshua had no idea how God would use Rahab in a major way to help him (Joshua 2).

But before that ever happened, Rahab had to surrender to God and recognize Him for who He is. Maybe that's you now? Maybe you have been doing things your own way for a while, and it isn't working. If you are ready to experience God's restoration power, then walk with me through Rahab's story as we uncover the four steps of The Rahab Rehab, which are: be ready, recognize, request, and be released.

Step 1—Be Ready for Rehab

When Joshua sent two spies from Shittim, they entered Jericho and stayed with Rahab. But the king of Jericho learns that spies have entered the land, so he sends a message to Rahab, telling her to send the men to him. Instead, Rahab helps the men escape by hiding them under the stalks of flax on the rooftop (Joshua 2:1–6).

How did Rahab orchestrate such a plan so quickly? The answer is: she didn't. This was no quickly executed plan. She was ready!

In reality, it seems that Rahab was a skilled businesswoman and that to label her a mere prostitute is an insult. The text states the spies came to *her* house to lodge there (Joshua 2:1 KJV), which implies she was a woman of means. She was no sex worker; she owned the joint.

And as such, you can bet she was shrewd and could identify ways to get ahead by just being attentive. As a woman of her profession, she found there were certain secrets or information that her guests were willing to share. In other words, even in the downstairs portion of the establishment, there were a variety of conversations—everything from "How's your day?" to debates about the current political climate—going on.

It is possible Rahab learned of Joshua's plan through the men who frequented her place of business before the king ordered her to send the spies to him. Armed with this information, Rahab didn't wait until the spies came to get ready. She stayed ready. She was on the lookout for her miracle, and she was ready.

You see, like Rahab, we can't get ready when we expect God to move. We've got to stay ready. How many of us are ready for a change in our lives? Are we sitting on the ready, expecting a breakthrough? Are we truly ready for an unexpected encounter, an outpouring of the Spirit?

Rahab was ready when the spies came. She was ready

with her "for the king" story—the lie she would tell the king when he asked where the spies were; she had the hideout ready, and she had the escape route ready. When she knew her change was coming, she was ready!

Thus when Rahab saw the window of opportunity, she seemed to act in a way that showed she thought, "*Why serve men when I can serve the true and living God?*" So, when the spies came knocking, she was ready for a rehab, she was ready for a change. Not only was she ready for it, but she was also open to it.

Are you open to rehab and ready for new opportunities? When the boss comes spying around your office, are you ready for the promotion? When someone new comes around, needing a friend, are you ready for the relationship? When an exciting opportunity drops into your lap, are you ready to take the leap? Surrendering is voluntary. Don't wait to be captured; make your move now!

Later in the story, we learn the soldiers "set out in pursuit of the spies on the road that leads to the fords of the Jordan, and as soon as the pursuers had gone out, the gate was shut" (Joshua 2:7 NIV). This has significance for us as well. Once we decide to surrender to God's will and serve wherever He sees fit to place us, He begins to shut the gate on some things in our lives, which further helps us in our rehab to recognize who God is.

Step 2—Recognize Who God Is

It's likely that Rahab grew up worshiping other gods and not really knowing the God of Israel. But when she heard about the Israelites and the God they served, she knew He was the one true God.

Thus, Rahab was not only ready with her plan; she also fully recognized who God was. As we read in her biblical account, she invited the spies into her home and told them she knew God had given them the land, and, because she had heard all that God had done for the Israelites, she was willing to do whatever it took to help them escape (Joshua 2:8–11).

The Bible does not say God did anything for Rahab at this point, yet she still recognized His power. She told the spies in Joshua 2:11, "When we heard of it, our hearts melted in fear and everyone's courage failed because of you, for the LORD your God is God in heaven above and on the earth below" (NIV).

I like Rahab because she was able to exalt God based solely on what she heard about Him. She told the spies, "When we heard of it, our hearts melted." So often, as it says in Romans 10:17, "faith comes by hearing, and hearing by the word of God" (NKJV).

How many of us can worship God simply because of what we heard? God may not have healed our bodies, but we heard what the Mighty Physician did for the woman across the street, just like the centurion in the New Testament had heard of Jesus and came for the healing of his sick daughter.

This is why it's so important to share our testimony with others. Someone may not be able to come to church, but they can *hear* about what God did for you, they can hear how God turned your life around, they can hear how you got saved.

I am reminded of the two criminals who were led along with Jesus to be put to death on the cross (Luke 23:32–43). They heard Jesus when He prayed for those crucifying Him, "Father, forgive them for they do not know what they do" (Luke 23:34 NKJV). We cannot know for sure, but perhaps hearing this is what softened the heart of one of the criminals.

That thief was on his way out; death was imminent when he heard, "Father, forgive them," and realized his chance for redemption. Something perked up in his spirit. He began to block out all the haters and heard Jesus for himself. And he said, "Lord, remember me when You come into Your kingdom" (Luke 23:42 NKJV).

When we hear about God and recognize Him for who He is, we know something in our life must change. Can you surrender to God based solely on what you hear? Can you *trust* God based solely on what you hear?

It's one thing to hear what other people say, but when you hear Jesus for yourself, something changes. There's a shift! When you hear Jesus for yourself, your attitude changes and your situation changes. You no longer think the way you used to think or feel the way you used to feel. You talk differently, and you walk differently.

Rahab may have been raised in Jericho worshiping false gods, but she knew the real God when she heard about Him. Others may doubt God, but we, who have heard so much about Him, cannot doubt Him. Because of her belief in God's power and who He is, Rahab wasn't a prisoner of war. In fact, she prospered in war by making a bold request.

Step 3—Request

Once you know who God is, you will have no problem making a request.

If I could, I would change the name of the Book of Joshua to the Bold and the Beautiful. Just when you think Rahab can't get any bolder, she has the faith and courage to make a request for her family: "Now then, please swear to me by the LORD that you will show kindness to my family because I have shown kindness to you. Give me a sure sign that you will spare the lives of my father and mother, my brothers and sisters, and all who belong to them—and that you will save us from death" (Joshua 2:12–13 NIV).

She didn't ask for a seat in the kingdom, or to be Joshua's wife, though they could have been a power couple. She didn't ask for power, wealth, or status, or to come out of hiding and be someone. All she asked for was salvation. In a sense, she was pleading, "All I want when this war is over is to be still alive. I don't want to die in this war. All I'm asking is for you to save me!"

And here is where salvation is all that matters. It's as if God guides us along the path of life in this way:[37]

- If your request is wrong, God says, "No."
- If the timing is not right, God says, "Slow."
- If you are wrong, God says, "Grow."
- But if you are right, the request and timing are right, God says, "Go!"

God granted Rahab's request because she was right, as nothing could be more right than wanting to be saved. Rahab knew what mattered and kept her attention focused on that.

However, there was an outward condition to this request for salvation. In verse 18, we see the spies' request for Rahab to place a scarlet cord in the window like a visible action of her faith.

Here is what's great about Rahab: not only did she make a request, but she also put some action behind her request. We've got to put action behind our prayers because faith without works is dead.

Philippians 4:6 reminds us that "by prayer and supplication with thanksgiving let your requests be made known to God" (ESV). Rahab did her part while she waited for God to do His part. And her part was so easy, so small. All she was instructed to do was gather her family inside her house and hang a scarlet rope in her window.

What small things has God been instructing you to do, but you keep putting them off?

God wants to bless you with the job—but have you

written your resume?

God wants you to be healthy—but have you gone to the gym?

God wants you to have a car—but have you taken your road test?

One act of obedience could save your life! This one act of obedience changed Rahab's whole life. This one act of surrender also saved her entire family. With a single act of obedience, Rahab went from deserving a scarlet letter on her person to hanging a scarlet cord in the window.

Lest you think this cord is just some rope to be grasped for safety, please understand it is highly symbolic. This scarlet cord was a symbol of holding on, which we sometimes must do when we make a request of God. Rahab's scarlet cord was a sign to the Hebrew armies to spare her family because she did not put her faith in man, but rather put her faith in God.

The scarlet rope—the color of blood—worked for Rahab just as much as the blood of the Passover lamb had worked during the exodus, where every home marked with blood was spared death that night (Exodus 12:13).

Don't miss the color of the rope. God's mercy and forgiveness toward Rahab were signified by a rope of scarlet thread, which becomes a symbol of the blood of Christ.

And we must realize no one gave Rahab the rope. God didn't give her the rope. Joshua didn't give her the rope. Rahab already had the rope. This signifies that we already have everything we need for God to bless us.

Also, the scarlet cord symbolizes her connection to Christ. When we read about the lineage of Jesus in Matthew 1:5, we discover that Rahab had married Salmon, and together, they had Boaz. Boaz married Ruth and had Obed, and Obed had Jesse, the father of David. David had Solomon, and so it continues. We go through a whole list of names in the lineage until we get to Jacob, who had Joseph, who was espoused to Mary, of whom Jesus was born.

This was no ordinary scarlet cord. It was an umbilical cord connecting Rahab to Jesus!

Life may get hard sometimes, but we must hold on to His Word, hold on to His Promise, and hold on to God's unchanging hand. We must hold on until our request for change arrives.

Step 4—Be Released

After we make the request for salvation, we must be released to wait for God to do the work. And after having been obedient, it was time for Rahab's release, although not immediately. Rahab's release was imminent but not immediate. Some time—four chapters in the book of Joshua to be exact—had passed since Rahab was made the promise of protection for her family. Rahab and her family were forced to wait.

While Rahab was waiting, God was working His plan through Joshua. God had given Joshua instructions in giving orders to the people: "When you see the ark of the covenant of the LORD your God, and the Levitical priests carrying it, you are to move out from your positions and follow it. Then you will know which way to go, since you have never been this way before" (Joshua 3:3–4 NIV).

And I believe that just when Rahab began to get weary, when the bright-red hue of the cord hanging from her window had paled to mauve from being bleached by the sun, when the cord's thick strands had begun to wither with every passing wind, and when waiting any longer seemed impossible, God made His move. Joshua 6:1–5 (ESV) says:

> *Now Jericho was shut up inside and outside because of the people of Israel. None went out, and none came in. And the LORD said to Joshua, "See, I have given Jericho into your*

> *hand, with its king and mighty men of valor. You shall march around the city, all the men of war going around the city once. Thus shall you do for six days. Seven priests shall bear seven trumpets of rams' horns before the ark. On the seventh day you shall march around the city seven times, and the priests shall blow the trumpets. And when they make a long blast with the ram's horn, when you hear the sound of the trumpet, then all the people shall shout with a great shout, and the wall of the city will fall down flat, and the people shall go up, everyone straight before him."*

And as forty thousand Israelites marched around the city, Rahab could feel the thunderous pounding of footsteps on the sandy ground. As the soldiers marched in unison, it not only intimidated their enemies, but it also gave Rahab a confidence boost.

And, I believe, Rahab's confidence in God grew stronger with every step she heard. She couldn't see the change, but she could feel God was making a move. We can't always see what God is doing in our lives, but we can, at times, feel the shift.

The longer the Israelite soldiers circled the wall, the more bricks began to fall. We may have crumbling walls of our own—walls of poverty, addiction, suffering, and brokenness. We can indeed tear down those walls, experience the bricks falling, and let God rebuild as He releases us to do His work.

Perhaps as the bricks kept falling faster, you could hear Rahab saying, "My shout is on the way! My release is on the way!"

We read in Joshua 6:16 that on the seventh round, "when the priests had blown the trumpets, Joshua said to the people, 'Shout!'" (ESV). As soon as the people heard the sound of the trumpets, they raised a great shout, and the wall fell down flat (Joshua 6:20). Then, Joshua told the two spies to bring Rahab and her family out of the house.

They didn't only bring her out, but all who belonged to her, just as she had prayed (Joshua 6:22–23). Her mother came out, her father came out, her sister came out, her brother came out—all her kindred came out. God did this while Rahab was waiting!

Redemption in Waiting

Like Rahab, sometimes we're forced to wait as well, but that doesn't mean God has given up on us. God is going to bless you. However, just as there were things that God had to put in place so that Rahab and her family could be released, it may take time—just a chapter or two—to see the blessings.

God never does anything haphazardly or on a whim. Everything He does is carefully planned and orchestrated. He said in Jeremiah 29:11, "I know the plans I have for you ... plans to prosper you ... plans to give you hope and a future" (NIV). But to give us that release of hope and a future, we may have to wait.

God is doing several things while we are waiting. While you're waiting, God is positioning. "This is how you will know that the living God is among you and that he will certainly drive out before you the Canaanites, Hittites, Hivites, Perizzites, Girgashites, Amorites and Jebusites" (Joshua 3:10 NIV).

While you're waiting, God is conquering the enemy. As they were crossing the Jordan, God said to "tell them that the flow of the Jordan was cut off before the ark of the covenant of the LORD. When it crossed the Jordan, the waters of the Jordan were cut off" (Joshua 4:7 NIV).

While you're waiting, God is moving and cutting some things off: "...everything the LORD had commanded Joshua was done by the people, just as Moses had directed Joshua. The people hurried over, and as soon as all of them had crossed, the ark of the LORD and the priests came to the other side while the people watched" (Joshua 4:10–11 NIV).

While you're waiting, God is healing. "The LORD said to Joshua, 'Today I have rolled away from you the disgrace of Egypt'" (Joshua 5:9 NRSV).

In other words, while you're waiting for a release, God is redeeming you and your story just as much as He redeemed Rahab and her story!

As we wait for God to do rehab work in our life, God is positioning things into place, conquering the enemy, healing, and redeeming you. Take heart—your release is coming! All you have to do is wait for it.

With that great comfort, we don't have to worry about what's happening in the current chapter of our lives because God is still writing our story. Like Rahab, can we believe God in Chapter 6 for what He had promised us in chapter 2? God is the author and finisher of our faith (Hebrews 12:2); we simply have to hang on to that scarlet cord of trust.

Then, when God brings us out, everything associated with us is coming out too. Your husband or wife and children are coming out.

In Rahab's rehab, she conquers the four steps—readiness, recognition, request, and release. But, it was the four words the spies said to her that meant the most: "Our life for yours" (Joshua 2:14 NRSV).

If we are ready and willing for rehab, Jesus is saying to us, "My life for yours; My pain for yours; My weakness for yours; My deliverance for yours; My dignity for yours; My blood for yours; My salvation for you; My eternity for yours."

Jesus surrendered His life, His blood, and the privileges of His divinity for us (Philippians 2:6–11). Now we have the privilege to tell the story, to be ready, and to be released!

WORKBOOK

Chapter Five Questions

Question: What "prisons" or "addictions" in your life—whether literal or figurative (such as faulty thinking or bad habits)—have left you in need of rehab? Is there damage that has been done to you by others that has left you in need of rehabilitation?

_____
_____
_____
_____
_____
_____
_____
_____
_____
_____

Question: Do you live ready for God to work in your life and to accept new opportunities He sends your way? How can you prepare your heart and life to be always ready for His divine intervention and encounters?

_____

_____

_____

_____

_____

_____

_____

_____

Question: Has it been difficult for you to wait on the Lord? Why? What attitude do you want to cultivate to strengthen you during a waiting season? (See Psalm 37; Isaiah 40:30–31; Romans 4:18–21.) How can you be more active than passive in your waiting?

_____

_____

_____

_____

_____
_____
_____
_____
_____
_____

Journal:
If the request is wrong, God says, "No."
If the timing is wrong, God says, "Slow."
If you are wrong, God says, "Grow."
But if you are right, the request and timing are right, God says, "Go!"

Thinking about this, look back at prayers you have prayed throughout your Christian journey. When have you seen each of these answers? How does this encourage you regarding prayers that seem to be "unanswered" now?

Action: Rahab had to act in faith to see God grant her deliverance. What small step of obedience is God asking you to take in the situations where you are asking Him to work? How will you get busy with what you can do while you wait for His deliverance?

Chapter Five Notes

CHAPTER SIX

Go For Yours

> *The daughters of Zelophehad are right in what they are saying; you shall indeed let them possess an inheritance among their father's brothers and pass the inheritance of their father on to them. You shall also say to the Israelites, "If a man dies, and has no son, then you shall pass his inheritance on to his daughter. If he has no daughter, then you shall give his inheritance to his brothers. If he has no brothers, then you shall give his inheritance to his father's brothers. And if his father has no brothers, then you shall give his inheritance to the nearest kinsman of his clan, and he shall possess it. It shall be for the Israelites a statute and ordinance, as the LORD commanded Moses."*
> —**Numbers 27:7–11** *(NRSV)*

Growing up in the great borough of Brooklyn, we had a saying on the streets, "Go for yours," which simply meant that when you saw an opportunity to get what you wanted, you went for it.

If a guy took an interest in a pretty girl walking by, his friends would say, "Go for yours." If you saw someone with whom you had a beef in the street, your friends might compel you to confront that person and "Go for yours!"

The last piece of chocolate cake is on the table: "Go for yours."

Daughters of Zelophehad

In the book of Numbers, God provides us with a beautiful example of what it means to "go for yours" in the daughters of Zelophehad. Zelophehad had five daughters: Mahlah, Noah, Hoglah, Milcah, and Tirzah (Numbers 27:1–2). He had no sons (27:4). Zelophehad is part of the generation of Israelites who departed from Egypt under Moses' leadership and who died during the forty years in the desert.

Now, although Zelophehad belonged to the old generation, his five daughters belonged to the new generation that would enter and possess the Promised Land. Up until this point, the Hebrew law only gave sons the right to the inheritance.

The daughters of Zelophehad recognized a problem for their family because their father was survived only by daughters, who were not eligible to inherit part of the promised Canaan land. Realizing their father would be posthumously punished, they asked for their inheritance early to perpetuate his memory (27:3–4).

These women had the courage to go against tradition and seek what was rightfully theirs. Unlike the generation before them, who were afraid to take hold of the Promised Land, these sisters learned from the faux pas of the previous generation. So, they stepped out, risking possible rejection or denial.

There was no precedent for the actions of these sisters—coming and requesting their inheritance. It was simply unheard of. I also find it ironic that their story is chronicled in the book of Numbers, yet they did not count. Women in those times were treated little more than personal possessions and were completely reliant upon men.

They had no rights and they had no voice. They weren't even counted whenever a census was taken. But we are about to see God give them a voice and an inheritance.

These five women challenged the system; they challenged the status quo because they saw their opportunity and *went for theirs*!

And God saw something special in these women because they are mentioned not once, not twice, but three times in the Bible. And not only are they mentioned, but they're also mentioned very specifically by name throughout Numbers. This tells us that even if you never count for something in people's eyes, you can rest assured you count for something with God. You are someone in God's sight.

These five beautiful, bodacious women were on the cusp of entering the Promised Land. Their desert experience was ending, and they were right on the edge of Canaan. They were about to come into their inheritance.

An inheritance is a property or possession that rightfully belongs to you, whether passed down legally or through family; it belongs to you. It's yours!

Perhaps that's exactly where you are. Maybe you are in a new season of your life with an inheritance before you. Maybe you are looking at a dream deferred that is coming to pass, or maybe you are expecting that promotion. In these new seasons of our lives, there are two mindsets: inheritance and acceptance.

But here's the difference between those two mindsets: one accepts what you're given, and the other reaches out for what you know you deserve.

To obtain your inheritance, you must be willing to go for yours! This is our window of opportunity, and like these women, we'll have to fight for it, we'll have to challenge the system, and we may even lose some people along the way. But this is the time to go for yours. And you must act now.

That's what I like about these five sisters—they were proactive, not reactive. Notice they did not wait until they arrived at the Promised Land to make their request known. No, they made their request before they even stepped one foot into the Promised Land.

They did not wait to accept whatever was given to them; they claimed their inheritance before it came to be and said: "Nah, I'm going to go for mine." They didn't have an acceptance mindset; rather, they had an inheritance mindset.

You don't have to wait until next year to claim your inheritance. You don't have to wait until everything is perfect. You don't even have to wait until you get yourself together. You can make your requests right now, even in a desert.

A Journey Through the Desert

Sometimes, though, you have to go through the desert before you can reach for the inheritance of what's been promised to you. But once your desert experience is over, you're about to go into the Promised Land. When we look at the story of these sisters and all that transpired, we realize the desert experience was only preparation for what God was about to do.

You can't appreciate the sunshine without rain, and you can't appreciate the Promised Land without the desert. You won't be able to appreciate this new season without everything you went through in the last one. That was your time of preparation. Before any great move in life, there is always a preparation period. Before David became king, he was prepared in the desert (1 Samuel 23:29). Before Jesus began His public ministry, He was prepared in the desert (Matthew 4:1–11).

Understand that each one of these women, the five sisters, went through the desert experience *with* their father,

Zelophehad. They were born in the desert, and, as a result, he named each one of them specifically for what he was experiencing in the desert at that time.

And just as the girls traveled with their father, so we travel with our Father. We don't have to go at it alone through the desert. No matter where we go, God knows our name and is with us. The meanings of these five sisters' names were significant for different things.

Mahlah means disease.[38] When Zelophehad named her, it's possible she was a sickly baby. But her name also means weak, grieved, wounded, sore, and tired.

Maybe your year has held a lot of sickness and pain. Maybe you were wounded by a break up, distraught over a job loss, or maybe you were grieved by the death of a loved one. Perhaps you were overworked, overburdened, and overstressed.

Well, for all the hurts and pain, you can claim an inheritance of healing in this new season of your life because God says, "I am the LORD that healeth thee" (Exodus 15:26 KJV).

Noah means motion.[39] I am sure this was Zelophehad's nod to the constant moving and wandering he had to do in the desert as they moved from camp to camp, putting up and breaking down tents. Having to do this for forty years was surely exhausting.

Maybe that's you today. Perhaps life has taken you places this year that you never thought you'd be. Or, maybe every time you build yourself up, something brings you back down again. And no matter what you do, you just can't seem to get settled. You've been wandering aimlessly through life, and all you want in this new season is some stability.

You had it all mapped out, but God took you in another direction, and He promises, "So do not fear, for I am with you, do not be dismayed, for I am your God, I will strengthen you and help you; I will uphold you with my righteous right hand" (Isaiah 41:10 NIV).

Hoglah means partridge, which is synonymous with quail.[40] Zelophehad was probably thinking of all the manna and quail God provided in the desert for His people to eat. It wasn't the best meal, and it wasn't always what they wanted, but it was always just enough.

Maybe you didn't get a new car, a new job, or lots of money. Maybe you've been wearing the same shoes and pressing the same suit for over a year. Maybe God hasn't given you everything you wanted. But what He did give you is always just enough.

Every time you went to the cupboard, there was a little flour left. Every time you looked in your wallet, there was a dollar in there that wasn't there before. You had just enough to make a living. Your rent is still paid. The heat is still on, and the water is still running. You still have clothes on your back, breath in your lungs, articulation of speech, and the activity of your limbs.

God may not have given you everything you wanted, but He, sure enough, gave you everything you need! Jesus said, "I am the bread of life. Whoever comes to me will never go hungry, and whoever believes in me will never be thirsty" (John 6:35 NIV).

Milcah means counsel.[41] By this time, Zelophehad was making the best of what was probably perceived as a bad situation. Being a man with no sons and four daughters, I am sure he questioned God and sought His counsel about his inability to have a son.

Perhaps you've sought God for some answers, as there were some things you were presented with that you just don't understand. Maybe you're not where you thought you'd be at this stage in life.

Even if you don't understand what God is doing and while it's not what you would have chosen for yourself, you must be encouraged by Proverbs 3:5: "Trust in the

LORD with all your heart and lean not on your own understanding..." (NIV). Proverbs also tells us in verse 6, "In all your ways submit to him, and he will make your paths straight"—so we can rest in that counsel.

Tirzah means [42] By the time his fifth and final daughter was born, Zelophehad named her Tirzah, which means pleasantness. At this stage, I believe Zelophehad had come to terms with his life. He would never have sons.

And I believe he looked back over his desert experience and realized that through it all, God still blessed him, fed him, and kept him, and for that, no matter what, he would delight himself in the Lord. And when you do that, God "shall give you the desires of your heart" (Psalm 37:4 NKJV).

So, as you look over your past, no matter what it was or what it wasn't—regardless of the hurt, pain, loss, discomfort, or highs and lows—God is still good!

I can testify that through it all, God is still good. God is still a keeper, and the same way He kept you through this hard or challenging season is the same way He'll keep you through the next.

Whatever your desert journey has been, God has been with you and prepared you along the way, and He has your inheritance ready for you. But you must take action to claim it.

Show Up

Well, if you're ready to claim your inheritance, the first thing you must do is show up. The daughters of Zelophehad showed up. Showing up was a risk, though. As women, conventional thinking at the time would have deemed it probably safer or more appropriate to send their message with a male clan member. They could've written a note and sent it to the tent meeting.

But the sisters chose not to send a note; instead, they

simply showed up. This teaches us that when it comes to your inheritance, it's something you must claim for yourself. No one can claim it for you, and no one can take it away from you. What God has for you is for you.

Many people want what God has for them, but they don't want to show up to claim it. But getting an inheritance from God is like winning a sweepstakes where you must be present to claim the prize.

And it's not just that the sisters showed up but where they showed up: at the tent of meeting, or the church. If you expect a paycheck, you show up for work; if you want some food, you show up at the grocery store. If you want your father's inheritance, you show up at your father's house. If you want something from God, your presence ought to be felt in His presence because this is where the inheritance is.

And it's not just about your physical presence but also about your spiritual presence. Another way to show up is to draw near. Drawing near to God is spending time with Him in prayer and His Word. The psalmist tells us, "The LORD is near to all who call upon Him, to all who call upon Him in truth" (Psalm 145:18 NASB).

The daughters came in a spirit of worship and exaltation for God. Before they even requested their inheritance, they were thankful for what God had already done for them and had given them. This speaks a lot about their relationship with God. And because they had a relationship with God, they trusted Him to provide the inheritance.

Think about all the stories you hear about wealthy people dying. Usually, the closest person to the deceased gets the biggest inheritance. The children come from far and wide expecting something only to have the will read and find that Daddy left everything to the dog. Why, that's because Fido was closest to them, and showed up with slippers and newspaper every time. His children did not draw near when they had the chance.

Though it may be a far-fetched illustration, it really holds true for us. If we draw near to God, He will draw near to us (James 4:8 ESV). These women showed up for their inheritance because not only did they have a relationship with their father, but they also had a relationship with *the* Father!

And that's important because once you show up, you have to be willing to finish the task. Their father was "the son of Hepher, the son of Gilead, the son of Makir, the son of Manasseh, belonged to the clans of Manasseh son of Joseph" (Numbers 27:1 NIV).

As such, these five sisters had to show Moses what they were made of because too much was on the line. They had to show Moses why they were the best people to receive this inheritance. No more manna and quail—these women had their eyes on the milk and honey.

It's About Your Family

The daughters of Zelophehad were "descendants of Hepher, Gilead, Makir, Manasseh, and Joseph." They came from good stock. Their father was a slave in Egypt, which means they knew the value of hard work. And, they came from the clan of Manasseh, a clan of warriors, which means they knew what it meant to fight. And their line went all the way to Joseph, which means that somewhere down the line, they were associated with royalty.

The experience of the Zelophehad daughters sounds a lot like the history of Blacks in America. We, too, are descendants of warriors and slaves who knew what it meant to fight. And when we go back a little further, there are some kings and queens in there, too—Nefatari, Musa, Shaka, and others. Black Americans stand on some mighty shoulders.

Sometimes people will look at you and assume they

have you pegged. So, every now and then, you may have to run down your resume of skills and strengths and remind people of who you are.

I am reminded of what Paul wrote in his second letter to the church in Corinth. Paul tells the Corinthians all about his heritage—the many times he was beaten for his faith, his shipwrecks, and being in danger with his own people simply because of who he was and for whom he stood (2 Corinthians 11:5–33). To get respect from the Corinthians, Paul had to show them what he was made of!

Likewise, remember when God answered Job? Job had gotten things twisted for a moment, and God had to remind him of who He was. God had laid the foundations of the Earth, hung the morning stars out to sing together, and told the oceans where its margins were (Job 38).

Occasionally, you've got to show them what you're made of! And not just what you're made of but *whose* you're made of.

And just in case they themselves weren't enough, these sisters began to explain who their father was. They essentially said, "Our father died in the wilderness. He wasn't part of Korah's anti-God gang. He died in his own sin" (Numbers 27:3). They wanted Moses to know that though he may have his doubts about them, their father was faithful.

Often, an inheritance has nothing to do with what you did but rather what your mama and daddy did. Our generation has education, opportunities, money, and success. We can look around and realize everything we have is because of the sacrifices they made. They were working long hours and wearing worn-out clothes, so we could have the best that money can buy. They had sleepless nights, "robbing Peter to pay Paul," so we could have a better life.

We need to thank God for the people who sacrificed so we could have an inheritance!

It's clear Zelophehad made some sacrifices for his children. He didn't associate with Korah (Numbers 27:3), though it would have been easy to rebel, given the forty-year situation in the desert. Instead, he persisted in following God so his girls could have better.

There are some things you can't receive on your own merit. Every once in a while, you may have to drop a name to get what you want. These women had to use their father's name.

So, just know, if you can't get your inheritance because of who you are, you can get it because of who your Father is. In Matthew, Jesus said of His Father: "...how much more will your Father who is in heaven give good things to those who ask Him" (Matthew 7:11 NKJV).

Not only do we have our Father, but we also have the name that is above every name (Philippians 2:9), Jesus. He said, "I will do whatever you ask in my name, so that the Father may be glorified in the Son" (John 14:13 NIV).

So we don't have to really tell anyone that a certain person sent us as they do in those old gangster movies: "Shorty sent me." We can tell them Jesus sent us, and the door will open because we know there is power in the name of Jesus!

When you show up and show them what you're made of, then God will show out!

Moses brought their case to God, who ruled, to paraphrase Numbers 27:6–7, "Zelophehad's daughters are right. Give them land as an inheritance among their father's relatives. Give them their father's inheritance."

These women had to appeal to Moses. I thank God we don't have to appeal to Moses today. I thank God that my inheritance is not based on what man says, but on how God rules. And because God rules, He can change the rules.

And when you are God's child, God will change the rules just for you! He changed the rules of anatomy when

He formed Adam from the dust of the ground. He changed the rules of ecology when he sent the ten plagues upon Egypt. He changed the rules of physics when He parted the Red Sea. He changed the rules of zoology when Daniel was in the lion's den. He changed the rules of chemistry for the boys in the fiery furnace. He changed the rules of biology when the Spirit came over Mary.

And if that weren't enough, one day God changed His own rules because we were beyond redemption until God sent His Son, Jesus. We serve a God who doesn't just make the rules; He can change the rules as we go for our inheritance!

WORKBOOK

Chapter Six Questions

Question: What is an area in your life where you want to try something you have never been done before? How can you muster the courage and boldness you need to take the next step, to be assertive instead of passive?

_____

_____

_____

_____

_____

_____

_____

_____

_____

_____

Question: When it comes to your future and your desires and dreams, do you have an acceptance mindset or an inheritance mindset? Who in the Bible demonstrates a reactive acceptance mindset? Who demonstrates a proactive inheritance mindset? What steps can you take to move from acceptance to inheritance thinking?

_____
_____
_____
_____
_____
_____
_____
_____
_____
_____

Question: Describe a desert experience you have been through on the way to seeing God's promises fulfilled. What did you learn from that situation and how can you apply that lesson to your life moving forward?

_____
_____
_____
_____

_____

_____

_____

_____

_____

_____

_____

_____

Journal: Journal about God's goodness in keeping you—in your heritage, in showing up and showing out—and *changing the rules* just for you.

Action: The five sisters each had a significant name. Do you know the meaning of your name? Learn what your name means, and ask God to give you a special understanding of the deeper spiritual message contained in your name and its meaning.

Chapter Six Notes

CHAPTER SEVEN

What's in Your Closet?

Therefore, as God's chosen people, holy and dearly loved, clothe yourselves with compassion, kindness, humility, gentleness and patience. Bear with each other and forgive one another if any of you has a grievance against someone. Forgive as the Lord forgave you. And over all these virtues put on love, which binds them all together in perfect unity.
—***Colossians 3:12-14***(NIV)

People love to dress up! It doesn't matter the nationality, age, or socioeconomic status, people—both male and female—love fashion and will go to extremes to curate the perfect ensemble.

Sometimes we sacrifice money, time, or relationships just so we can be fashionable. If we don't think the way we handle money matters, then some people will choose to forgo paying a bill in favor of the perfect pair of shoes. If we perceive time isn't important, then we take those opportunities to add to our wardrobe. I can recall waiting for my uncle to pick me up from the bus stop once, which happened to be in front of a department store. In the fifteen minutes it took for my uncle to arrive, I purchased two suits, a dress, *and* three ties for my husband—with five minutes to spare.

If we treat our relationships like they don't matter, then we bypass them to accrue more clothing. In a sermon by Stephen Evoy, he tells a story about a woman:[43]

> [She] promised her husband she would curb her shopping and stick to their budget. Well, that promise was short-lived because the very next day, the wife came home with a new dress. Furious, the husband said, "I thought we had an agreement." The wife stated that she just couldn't help herself. The temptation was too great. The husband said, "Well, you should have told Satan to get behind you." She said, "I did, and he said the dress looked even better from the back."

Oh yes, we can go to great lengths to look good on the outside, to impress people, and to raise our spirits. However, most times, we don't make the same effort to look as good on the inside. But God couldn't care less about your outfit. What really matters to God is your "in-fit."

As a child, I remember my mother giving me the famous clean underwear speech. You know: "Make sure you wear clean underwear in case you're in an accident." At the time, I thought that was ridiculous. I mean really; if you're in an accident, doesn't that take precedence over having on clean underwear?

But the more I thought about it as an adult, the more it made sense, and I realized what my mother was trying to say. You can appear, oh! so fabulous on the outside, but it's what's underneath that may embarrass you. What we're wearing on the outside only covers up our true selves underneath.

Wearing the Proper Clothing

The first-century women in 1 Timothy 2:9 went

through quite a process to get dressed and be beautiful. These women dressed in fine clothes, braided their hair or piled it in eccentric styles, and donned all sorts of bangles and beaded jewelry of necklaces, bracelets, rings, and earrings, just so they could have a gorgeous outward appearance.

Women today still seek the best make-up, designer jeans, and the latest fashions. Designers put their best new ideas out each season. Although God certainly wants us to be properly clothed, He isn't impressed with our outward appearance.

Since you are God's chosen model, if you are to be effective witnesses for Christ, you ought to be clothed properly, that is, spiritually clothed.

In Paul's letter to Colossae, his goal was to combat the false teachings that had infiltrated the Colossian church. The people began to combine other philosophies and religions with Christian truths.

And because Paul was concerned the people would be led into a relapse, he wrote this letter to remind them not to fall prey to false doctrines, which emphasized a life based on the promotion of man rather than a Christian life based upon a true understanding of the life and person of Christ.

Let me explain this in fashion terms. Instead of being trendsetters for Jesus, the Colossians were being trendy. And while trends may seem fun, they're only temporary. We tend to do the same thing. We fix our hearts on material things and appearance instead of building our hopes on things eternal.

Colossae was a textile city, meaning they specialized in fabric and materials,[44] so it's no surprise that Paul would speak to the Colossians in a language they could understand as he encouraged them to "clothe themselves." Paul was saying, in effect, "While you're out here dressing everyone else, there are a few patterns I need *you* to put into production for yourselves."

The Christians at Colossae were not called to wear the world's clothes, but to wear God's clothes. And we know God is a great designer; after all, aren't we fearfully and wonderfully made (Psalm 139:14 NIV)? Well, every designer needs a model. The Bible states, "Therefore, as God's chosen people, holy and dearly loved" (Colossians 3:12 NIV).

Models are invaluable to a designer. It is important to understand that models don't volunteer, but they are chosen—some for their height, some for their eyes, and some simply because they have "it." As God's models, we are also chosen. Ephesians 1:4 says, "For he chose us in him before the creation of the world" (NIV).

God's divine selection is not based on what we look like. His selection does not depend on anything we have, nor does it depend on anything we've done. Rather, God chooses us simply because He loves us.

When I was fourteen-years-old, my brother encouraged me to enter a beauty pageant. He was concerned I was too content to be a lazy teenager for the summer. He believed modeling would be a great outlet for me—anything to get me off the couch. To him, I had all the makings of a top model. But that did not help my confidence.

I can remember going to auditions and walking into a room full of girls who looked just like me. And I would think to myself, what is going to set me apart from all these other girls? But, thank God as His model, we don't have to worry about setting ourselves apart! God has already set us apart—that is the meaning of the word *holy*.[45]

Models must also be marketable. When something is marketable, that means the buyer wants that product. When you look through magazines, it's the model's job to make the garment appealing so that it attracts the buyer's attention. His smile, her figure, the wind blowing in their hair—the overall look makes you want to buy what they are selling.

As God's models, we too should be marketable. As a Christian, do people want what you're selling or promoting? Are you promoting peace? Joy? Faith? Our responsibility, our job is to display God and make being His follower and the relationship we have with God appealing to others.

Oh, by the way, my brother was right. I did win both the local and national titles and went on to compete for Miss New York USA.

Don't Forget the Fashion Makeover!

Before we can be successful as God's model and be appealing to others, we need a makeover. Everyone loves the makeover scene in the movies. You know the one where the funky music is playing, and she's tossing clothes out of the dressing room—the feel-good scene when the dowdy girl finally gets fixed up and we all cheer. Yet, in real life, sometimes getting a makeover isn't this exciting.

On the television show *America's Next Top Model*, women from all over the country compete for the top spot as the next "it girl."[46] And if you've ever seen the show, you know how passionate these women are. They are willing to do *anything* to win the contract and all that comes with it. They are willing to do anything except one thing: get a makeover!

The minute they are told to change their look or style, immediately, the screaming starts, and the tears flow. Some will even go as far as threatening to leave the show. The bottom line is this: these women want the prize, but they're not willing to change to get it.

Aren't we guilty of the same thing? We all want to be Christlike until it's time for a makeover. We're all in until we realize God requires us to look and act differently from what we're used to. Everyone wants to be Christlike until they find out what Christ is like. He loves everyone, forgives his enemies, and turns the other cheek (Matthew 5:39).

You can't be God's disciple without a makeover. So, what does this makeover consist of? Well, all you have to do is change your clothes. We must clothe ourselves with compassion, kindness, humility, gentleness, and patience.

Perhaps you already think you look pretty good and stylish on the outside. But, on the inside, some behaviors, emotions, and thought processes are seriously outdated. When you follow Christ, some things simply don't fit you anymore.

In Colossians 3, verse 8, Paul encourages us to get rid of the old, nasty garments we've been wearing. Paul says, "But now you must also rid yourselves of all such things as these: anger, rage, malice, slander, and filthy language from your lips" (NIV).

Isn't it time to clean out the closet? Once we realize we don't even have enough room for all the junk we have in there, we will gladly switch out for a new wardrobe that reflects Christ.

Now, it may be hard when we have to throw out our belongings, but Paul takes us to fashion week and shows that God's new collection is hot. Paul encourages us to put on new attire from the House of Colossians—The Closet Collection:

- A coat of compassion to share warmth with others in need.
- Kicks (slang for shoes) of Kindness, so as you run this Christian race, you're careful not to step on any toes along the way.

- A hat of humility, to protect your head from thinking you're higher than you ought.

- Gloves of gentleness to handle situations properly and with care.

- Pantyhose of patience, so when you feel like you're about to lose it, you have a garment to help you hold it all in.

Here's the best part: God didn't just give us one outfit. He gave us an entire wardrobe with an ensemble for every occasion. When in despair, you can head to Isaiah 61:3, and put on the garment of praise! Are you going into battle? Go to Ephesians 6:10–18 and put on the whole armor of God! With God, we can put on a new wardrobe of success that will certainly make a statement to others. But, we need to make the right statement!

Complete Your Garments

To be a successful model, not only do you need a makeover, but you also need clothes that make a statement. If the Little Black Dress (LBD) is the world's fashion go-to, then love is the Christian's fashion go-to. As the Bible says, "And over all these virtues put on love, which binds them all together in perfect unity" (Colossians 3:14 NIV).

Nothing makes a bigger statement than love. You see, at this point, you have on some great accessories, but your outfit is not complete without love.

Love not only binds all the virtues together to complete the garment of Christian character, but it also binds the members of the church together in perfect unity. The church is about God's people serving together in perfect unity.

And when you dress in love, you're always dressed appropriately. Love is like a little black dress or basic black suit appropriate for any occasion. These are considered essential to a complete wardrobe because they can be dressed up or down, depending on the occasion.

Let me illustrate. Some time ago, my boss was invited to the world premiere of a new movie, and I desperately wanted to go. When I gave him his tickets, he mentioned he might not attend. So, on the day of the event, I purposely wore my LBD to work just in case. To my surprise, I was able to attend, and I was perfectly dressed for work that day and for the premiere that night.

That's what love is! When you wear love, you're always dressed for the occasion. I love the way The Message Bible explains love in Colossians 3:14, "And regardless of what else you put on, wear love. It's your basic, all-purpose garment. Never be without it."

This garment of love is vintage, as Jesus debuted it over two thousand years ago, and it's also an heirloom because He passed down love to us through forty two generations.

Love is never trendy; love is a classic that never goes out of style. In fact, when you wear love, you're the best-dressed person in the room. And no matter what the situation, love is always appropriate.

However, putting on love and all your accessories are not only a great ensemble, but they're also your spiritual uniform. In most professions, wearing a uniform is a requirement of the job. And if you are going to work for God as His model, then you are required to wear this uniform.

Uniforms are designed to identify you. For instance, when we see a man or woman in a blue uniform, we know they are a police officer, so we can seek safety. When I see a person wearing a big, white chef's hat, I know this person will take care of my meal needs. In contrast, your spiritual uniform should identify you, because after all, the Bible says people will know we are His disciples by the love we wear (John 13:35).

Not only do uniforms identify us, but uniforms are designed to protect us. Police wear bulletproof vests to protect them if they are shot. Firefighters wear a helmet to protect their heads from fire and from falling debris. And as Christians, we must wear our uniform of love to protect our relationships and us from the wiles of the enemy who desires to destroy us (John 10:10). Our uniform is not about fashion.

Wear Love Fashionably

Jesus knew all about fashion. We were made in the image of God, and our many garments were sewn by Jesus throughout the ages. The Bible says in Colossians 1:17 that "he is before all things, and in him all things hold together" (NIV).

Jesus came from heaven to earth in the flesh (John 1:14), which tells us He wasn't afraid of dressing down. Now, I'm a shoe lover, but Jesus wore some sandals that John wasn't even fit to tie (John 1:27). And Jesus was not afraid to wear prints, because we read in the Bible that by His stripes we are healed (Isaiah 53:5 NKJV). And He also understood the concept of a good hemline because when the woman with the issue of blood touched His garment hem, she was made whole (Matthew 9:20 KJV).

In addition, He's the ultimate stain remover, because only the blood of Jesus can wash away our sins (1 John 1:7). Therefore, Jesus wore a cross before it was ever fashionable to do so. And He wasn't afraid to wear red. As a matter of fact, He was covered in the crimson color as He hung on the cross and died for our sins.

Then He went away for three days to receive a makeover and got up with all power in His hands (Matthew

28:18 KJV). And now He's sitting at the right hand of God, watching His models serve on the runway of life.

When we choose to wear love, we don't have to worry about what the enemy throws at us because God's love is stain resistant. We don't worry about taking shots because God's love is bulletproof. We don't worry about being destroyed because God's love is unbreakable (Romans 8:38–39).

Like all good fashion, He's coming back (John 14:3)! So get your closet in order because He will be looking for a church without a spot or wrinkle (Ephesians 5:27)!

WORKBOOK

Chapter Seven Questions

Question: Describe a time when you sacrificed money, time, or even a relationship to look good on the outside. What sacrifices have you made to form beautiful character on the inside?

_____
_____
_____
_____
_____
_____
_____
_____
_____
_____
_____

Question: Instead of being *trendsetters* for Jesus, the Colossians were being *trendy*. What qualities does it take to be a trendsetter? How can you know if you are setting trends for Jesus or following the trends of this world?

_____

_____

_____

_____

_____

_____

_____

_____

_____

_____

Question: How does it change your attitude and actions to know you are already chosen and set apart by God simply because of His great love and what Christ has done for you? How are you doing in displaying God in a way that draws others to desire a relationship with Him?

_____

_____

_____

_____

_____

_____

_____

_____

_____

_____

_____

Journal: Everyone wants to be *Christlike* until they find out *what Christ is like*. What areas of Christlikeness do you find difficult to emulate? Journal about the ways you have already become more like Him and the areas where you need His "makeover."

Action: Look at the list of clothing a Christian should put on. Choose one you most need in your life now and study that quality in greater depth. Then write down three concrete, practical ways you can begin to work on it.

Chapter Seven Notes

CONCLUSION

A Prayer for My Sister

Father, I come to You today in the name of Jesus. I come to You with a heart of humility and in the spirit of unity and reconciliation, Lord.

Today, I stand before You God, in the presence of my sister. Though we may not be related by the blood of our parents, we are related by the blood of Jesus Christ.

Today, I affirm my sister and pray You strengthen her when she is weak, give her wisdom in the midst of confusion, and give her peace in the midst of chaos.

Today, I rejoice with my sister and thank You for the great things You are doing in her life. Thank You for her success, thank You for her triumphs, and thank You for bringing her through trials with a greater purpose and understanding of Your might. Most of all, I praise You in advance for the great things that are to come.

Today, I grieve with my sister. We know that all things work together for good (Romans 8:28), but until the good is realized, I grieve with my sister. Lord, carry her through any loss she has suffered. Comfort her through the heartbreaking moments of life and heal her of any sickness that may threaten her health and well-being. And when she needs support, give other sisters the compassion to offer her a shoulder to cry on, a hand to hold, and ears to listen.

Today, I agree with my sister. Father, help us to walk in agreement with each other. Teach us to be slow to speak and quick to listen (James 1:19). And when we do speak, let the words of our mouths and the meditation of our hearts be acceptable in thy sight (Psalm 19:14) and edifying, encouraging, and uplifting to my sister.

Today, I will work in harmony with my sister to build this body of Christ. Remind us that when we come to Your house, it is our responsibility to uplift Your kingdom. Father, help me not to do anything out of selfish ambition or vain conceit, but to act out of humility, valuing my sister above myself (Philippians 2:3).

Today, I remind my sister that she is loved and fearfully and wonderfully made (Psalm 139:14). Thank You, Father, for this beautiful woman reading this book who gives of herself so freely.

Thank You, for the competency she gives to the workplace, and thank You for the joy she gives to her loved ones. Thank You for the comfort and stability she gives to her family. Thank You for the guidance she gives those who look up to her and the hope she gives to those she looks up to, and thank You for the pride she gives to her parents. Thank You for the laughter she gives to her friends, and thank You for the gifts she gives to this church. And above all, thank You for the praise she gives to You.

Father, thank You for *her*. Amen!

About the Author

Rev. Tisha Dixon-Williams serves as pastor of the First Baptist Church of Bridgehampton in Bridgehampton, New York. A Brooklyn native, and a gifted and natural communicator, she is the Creator and Chief Curator of the global women's ministry movement Who's That Lady? Ministries.

REFERENCES

Notes

[1] Marlowe, Christopher. *Doctor Faustus.* 1.13. The Harvard Classics, 1909, p. 88–89. In Bartleby.com. https://www.bartleby.com/19/2/.

[2] Schroeder, Allison and Theodore Melfi. *Hidden Figures.* Directed by Theodore Melfi. Fox 2000 Pictures, 2016.

[3] Lockyer, Herbert. "Mary Magdalene." *All the Women of the Bible.* Zondervan, 1988. In Bible Gateway. com. https://www.biblegateway.com/resources/all-women-bible/Mary-Magdalene.

[4] "The Role of Women." Bible History Online. https://www.bible-history.com/jesus/jesusThe_Role_of_Women.htm.

[5] Lawrence, Donald. "Healed." *I Speak Life.* Sony Legacy, 2004.

[6] Borland, James A. "How Jesus Viewed and Valued Women." Crossway, 2017. https://www.crossway.org/articles/how-jesus-viewed-and-valued-women/.

[7] Lockyer, Herbert. "Joanna." *All the Women of the Bible*. Zondervan, 1988. In Bible Gateway. https://www.biblegateway.com/resources/all-women-bible/Joanna.

[8] Lockyer, Herbert. "Susanna." *All the Women of the Bible*. Zondervan, 1988. In Bible Gateway. https://www.biblegateway.com/resources/all-women-bible/Susanna.

[9] Rivera, Christopher. "#TBT EDCLV Edition: Flosstradamus– Total Recall." EDM Identity. June 15, 2017. https://edmidentity.com/2017/06/15/tbt-edc-flosstradamus-total-recall/.

[10] Gill, John. "1 Samuel 1." *Exposition of the Entire Bible*. In Internet Sacred Text Archive. https://www.sacred-texts.com/bib/cmt/gill/index.htm.

[11] Giordano, Connie. "Compensation for Lack." Walking in Truth. http://www.walkingintruth.org/Walkingintruth/devotions/wit2007/april2007/wit043007.htm.

[12] Strong, James. "H639 – 'aph." *Strong's Exhaustive Concordance of the Bible*. Hunt & Eaton, 1894. In Blue Letter Bible. https://www.blueletterbible.org/lang/lexicon/lexicon.cfm?Strongs=H639&t=KJV.

[13] Day, Suzanne. "Brain "Rewires" Itself to Enhance Other Senses in Blind People." EurekAlert. March 22, 2017. https://www.eurekalert.org/pub_releases/2017-03/meae-bi031717.php.

[14] Hitchcock, Roswell D. "Entry for 'Peninnah.'" *An Interpreting Dictionary of Scripture Proper Names*. 1869. In

Bible Study Tools. https://www.biblestudytools.com/dictionary/peninnah/.

[15] Strong, James. "H4672 – matsa'." *Strong's Exhaustive Concordance of the Bible*. Hunt & Eaton, 1894. In Blue Letter Bible. https://www.blueletterbible.org/lang/lexicon/lexicon.cfm?Strongs=H4672&t=KJV.

[16] Mariottini, Claude. "Who Was King Lemuel?" May 18, 2009. Dr. Claude Mariottini—Professor of Old Testament. https://claudemariottini.com/2009/05/18/who-was-king-lemuel/.

[17] "What Oprah Knows for Sure About Finding Strength After Betrayal." Oprah.com. https://www.oprah.com/omagazine/strength-after-a-betrayal-oprah.

[18] Obama, Michelle. *Becoming*. United States: Crown, 2018.

[19] Rhimes, Shonda. *Year of Yes: How to Dance It Out, Stand In the Sun and Be Your Own Person*. Simon & Shuster, 2015.

[20] Henry, Frederick. "Secret of a Happy Marriage–'Crocheting Dolls.'" Catholic Diocese of Calgary. December 4, 2013. http://www.calgarydiocese.ca/news-events/bishops-blog/secret-of-a-happy-marriage-crocheting-dolls.html.

[21] *Random House Unabridged Dictionary*, "conflict." In Dictionary.com. https://www.dictionary.com/browse/conflict.

[22] Mowczko, Margaret. "Women Leaders in the Philippian Church." CBE International. 2011. https://www.cbeinternational.org/blogs/women-leaders-philippian-church.

[23] Strong, James. "G2137 – euodoō." *Strong's Exhaustive Concordance of the Bible*. Hunt & Eaton, 1894. In Blue Letter

Bible. https://www.blueletterbible.org/lang/lexicon/lexicon.cfm?t=kjv&strongs=g2137.

[24] Strong, James. "G2137 – euodoō." *Strong's Exhaustive Concordance of the Bible*. Hunt & Eaton, 1894. In Blue Letter Bible. https://www.blueletterbible.org/lang/lexicon/lexicon.cfm?strongs=G2137&t=KJV.

[25] Strong, James. "G4941 – Syntychē'." *Strong's Exhaustive Concordance of the Bible*. Hunt & Eaton, 1894. In Blue Letter Bible. https://www.blueletterbible.org/lang/lexicon/lexicon.cfm?strongs=G4941&t=KJV.

[26] Strong, James. "G4940 – syntygchanō." *Strong's Exhaustive Concordance of the Bible*. Hunt & Eaton, 1894. In Blue Letter Bible. https://www.blueletterbible.org//lang/lexicon/lexicon.cfm?Strongs=G4940&t=KJV.

[27] *Merriam-Webster.com Dictionary*, "beseech." Merriam-Webster. https://www.merriam-webster.com/dictionary/beseech.

[28] Weber, Stephen C. "True Yokefellows." Daily Encouragement. March 1, 2011. https://dailyencouragement.wordpress.com/category/religion/page/28/.

[29] Jones, E. Stanley. Quoted in *1001 Quotes, Illustrations, and Humorous Stories for Preachers, Teachers, and Writers*. Edited by Edward K. Rowell. Baker Books, 2008, p. 174.

[30] "The Messiah Is Among You." Stories for Preaching. https://storiesforpreaching.com/the-messiah-is-among-you/.

[31] Lemert, Charles. *Why Niebuhr Matters*. Yale University Press, 2011, p. 193.

[32] Lemert, *Why Niebuhr Matters*, p. 234.

[33] Lemert, *Why Niebuhr* Matters, p. 195.

[34] *Lexico*, "Rehabilitation." https://www.lexico.com/definition/rehabilitation.

[35] *Lexico*, "Rehabilitation."

[36] *Lexico*, "Rehabilitation."

[37] Hybels, Bill and LaVonne Neff. *Too Busy Not to Pray: Slowing Down to Be With God.* Intervarsity Press, 1998, p. 88.

[38] Lockyer, Herbert. "Mahalah-Mahlah." *All the Women of the Bible.* Zondervan, 1988. In Bible Gateway. https://www.biblegateway.com/resources/all-women-bible/Mahalah-Mahlah.

[39] Strong, James. "H5270 – No`ah." *Strong's Exhaustive Concordance of the Bible.* Hunt & Eaton, 1894. In Blue Letter Bible. https://www.blueletterbible.org/lang/lexicon/lexicon.cfm?Strongs=H5270&t=KJV.

[40] Lockyer, Herbert. "Hoglah." *All the Women of the Bible.* Zondervan, 1988. In Bible Gateway. https://www.biblegateway.com/resources/all-women-bible/Hoglah.

[41] Lockyer, Herbert. "Milcah No. 1." *All the Women of the Bible.* Zondervan, 1988. In Bible Gateway. https://www.biblegateway.com/resources/all-women-bible/Milcah-No-1.

[42] Lockyer, Herbert. "Tirzah." *All the Women of the Bible.* Zondervan, 1988. In Bible Gateway. https://www.biblegateway.com/resources/all-women-bible/Tirzah.

[43] Evoy, Stephen. "I Heard a Story About a Woman...."

Sermon Central. Outreach Inc. https://www.sermoncentral.com/sermon-illustrations/64565/i-heard-a-story-about-a-woman-who-spent-all-day-by-stephen-evoy.

[44] Wilson, Ralph F. "Introduction to Colossians." JesusWalk. 2019. http://www.jesuswalk.com/colossians/0_intro.htm.

[45] Strong, James. "H6944 – qodesh." *Strong's Exhaustive Concordance of the Bible*. Hunt & Eaton, 1894. In Blue Letter Bible. https://www.blueletterbible.org/lang/lexicon/lexicon.cfm?Strongs=H6944&t=KJV.

[46] *America's Next Top Model*. Produced by Tyra Banks et al. CBS Television Distribution.

www.ingramcontent.com/pod-product-compliance
Lightning Source LLC
Chambersburg PA
CBHW071118160426
43196CB00013B/2617